POEMS:

BY

ELIZA GABRIELLA LEWIS.

Εγῶ ἀγαπουῦσα καλὴτερον.

Brooklyn:
PRINTED BY SHANNON & CO.,
98 Cranberry street.

1850.

CONTENTS.

PAGE.

The Outlaw, a Dramatic Sketch, ... 1
Can the voice die 55
Medora's Song 56
Song 58
Listening to the Music of the Telegraph Wires.. 60
Impromptu .... *ib.*
To the Absent 61
The love of other days 62
Stanzas 64
To Mary 66
Song 67
A Penitent's Address to the Muse 68
Love, Reason, and Truth 70
Song 71
To the Author of "A New Reading of Old Songs" 73

PAGE.
The Impatient 74
To die in summer's pride, alas! 76
Song 78
To R—— 80
"Winter with snow flakes on his hoary brow"... 81
Voice of the Thunder-Cloud 83
On a Violet.................................. 85
To Cora 86
Invocation.................................... 88
The Deserted Wife 89
To —— 91
Thoughts 92
To the Message Bird 93
The Exile's Lament 94
The Reverse.................................. 96
Song 97
To —— 98
Stanzas...................................... 99
To —— 101
Death of Opechancanough 102
To Grace 103

PAGE.

Love 104

Nay say not so, beloved 105

To ——— 106

Confessions.................................. 108

I'll dream no more 110

The Packet Ship Ashburton 111

The Coquette................................. 113

To the memory of one of the Signers of the Independence 115

Childhood's Prayer 117

The Consumptive.............................. 119

Philosophy of the Stars...................... 121

The Festival................................. 122

The "Bloody Run" 125

The Backwoodsman's Tale 128

The last errand of the Indian Chief "Bald Eagle" 134

The Blasted Oak 136

The Combat................................... 138

Death and the Warrior........................ 141

Queen Mary's escape from Lochleven Castle.... 143

To ——— 147

THE OUTLAW;

A DRAMATIC SKETCH.

DRAMATIS PERSONÆ.

DUKE MALVINO, *(Father of Lady Isabella).*

BARON ALBERTO RIVOLI.

BARONESS ISABELLA.

HELVITIO, THE OUTLAW, *(Lady Isabella's brother).*

LORD OSCAR, *(Friend of the Baron).*

AMELIA, } *Attendants of Lady Isabella.*
PAGE, }

JAILOR, SOLDIERS, CITIZENS, &c.

MOUNTAINEERS.

MADELINE, *(A mountain girl).*

OLD WOMAN.

GIRLS.

THE OUTLAW.

ACT. I.

SCENE I.—*Dungeon.*

HELVITIO *chained.*

Enter Jailor.

Jailor. SIX thousand marks, good master rob- ·, I think thou said'st, this morning?

Helvitio. Six thousand marks, old fellow; are they not a goodly ransom for these rusty chains?

Jail. Aye! but, my head! My head it sitteth now most firmly on my shoulders. Should'st thou escape, might I not tremble for it?

Hel. And should I not?—Six thousand marks die with me.

Jail. But wilt thou swear?—[*aside.*] What oath can hold a robber?—What pledge givest thou of this forthcoming ransom?

Hel. My word.

Jail. A goodly pledge, no doubt, and one most worthy; but——

Hel. Old man, I am an outlaw; yet I bear
A heart that throbs as thine hath never throbb'd;
And were my life a ransom for the falsehood,
I would, upon the scaffold, lay it down,
Rather than sully it—by a base lie!

Jail. Well, well! no need to put thee in a passion.
Five thousand marks are set upon thy head—
But that the soldiers who entrapp'd thee 'll share:—
So then, if thou wilt promise me, most truly,
To pay six thousand marks into my hands,
Three days at farthest, after thy release,
Our bargain's made.

Hel. I promise thee: Come, come, knock off the fetters!

Jail. Softly; I must file them off;
And to do that must get an instrument.
I will be with thee anon.
[*Exit* Jailor.

Hel. Now, by yon Heaven, I almost scorn my Freedom—
Bought from this traitorous knave!
Would that my own good sword could cleave
A passage through these walls.——
Man, it is said, hath ever
Some enduring passion for wealth, and state—
Power—fame—or love:
Each moveth different natures—such, not mine.
Oh! I would be the Eagle, in its flight
Soaring to Heaven and sunning its strong pinions
Beneath the glorious sun;
And when fatigued with gazing on its splendor,
My couch should be the high and rugged cliff,
Whose dangerous steep man never yet hath climb;
My food, torn from the pale and worthless slave,
Whose soul would grudge the given morsel;
And, for the music of the tinkling lyre,

Give me the mountain breeze—the sea-bird call—
The moaning of the chafed and angry waters.
——Caught thus, and caged,
Whilst sleep bedimmed my senses:
My band dispersed—roving I know not whither—
And fearful of their captains doom—
Death by the headsman's hand.
Courage, my heart, I hear my jailor's step,
And in that tread lieth freedom!

Enter Jailor.

Jail. Softly, softly; thou seem'st in angry mood.
Here is the cunning tool—now for thy fetters!
[*Files them.*] They're off.—I'll drop this file nigh by thy straw.
Thou'rt free; and here the rope—tie hands and feet;—
I will prove me innocent. Knock down the sentinel.
God speed! Yet hearken—the six thousand marks.
[*Exit* HELVITIO.

SCENE II.—*A Ruinous Castle by the Sea-shore —precipitous rocks—a small boat moored.*

Enter BARON ALBERTO *and* Page.

Page. Around this ruined castle oft, my Lord,
I've seen my lady wander; and the weary night
O'er-burthen with her sorrow.

B. Alber. Deem'st thou her love so perfect,
That the edge of this most doting passion
Still remains a dagger in her bosom?
Love's she him yet?

Page. My lord, of whom now speakest thou?

B. Alber. [*agitated with passion.*] Whom speak I of? Knave thou dost know
I know not whom I speak of—yet this much know:—
He has a serpent's tongue—a smooth and flowery speech—
Such winneth woman;—soft and fair
The curling moustache, and the clustering locks.
Ye marvel that I saw thus much, at such
A damning moment? Know then, I noted

With a jealous eye—one hungry for revenge—
And marked well, upon my bosom's tablets,
Each cozening trait.

Page. Oh, my lord, my lord!
I pray thee look not thus. [sir;

B. Alber. [*recovers himself.*] Speak on young
What of thy virtuous lady?

Page. For hours she leans 'gainst yonder battlement,
With eyes, that weeping, seem two precious gems,
Half hidden 'neath the pure and lucid wave,
That but enhance their beauty.
Believe me, noble sir, she mourns the loss
Of thy prized love most deeply.
I have seen true and honest grief:
My mother wept when my kind father died—
So weeps the gentle Lady Isabel.

B. Alber. [*musing.*] It seems as yesterday.
I see her now, with modest look,
Gazing upon my face—my own fair bride!
Was that a brow to write deceiver on?
Oh! woman, woman!

Page. [*kneeling.*] Pardon me, my Lord ;
I pray thee think it not.
Forgive my boldness :—see my gentle lady ;
It is the hour at which she's wont to walk :
Oh ! wilt thou not speak peace unto her bosom ?
Look on her form—wasted by gnawing care ;
Through her wan slender fingers glide the tears,
Forever flowing ;—I can ne'er believe
That guilt e'er dwelt with so much humbleness !

B. Alber. [*still musing.*] Who spoke of peace ?
Canst thou bestow such boon ?
Restore a wanton's purity—a husband's trust ?
God's blessing on thine head, if thou can'st do it :
But no—I tell thee she's as false as hell !
I saw the clasping hands—the speaking glance—
The tears that fell at parting ! Get thee gone,
Thou tempting devil !

Page. [*kneeling.*] One word—only one word—
Forgive——

B. Alber. Up, boy ; I have resolved to try
The lady's boasted constancy. My friends
Think me abroad—my rank concealed—

Engaged in foreign warfare:—Report my death,
And I will then retire to yonder cave,
And play the holy hermit; there I'll wait
'Till time hath proved suspicion true or false.—
Boy, thou must hence, and to thy lady say—
Alberto's dead; shed tears and counterfeit
True sorrow well.

Page. Poor lady, 'twill not need;
My tears fall truly for her.

B. Alber. Give her these papers and this signet ring;
This letter—my farewell: Tell her I died,
Forgiving her, upon the battle field.

[*Exit* Page.

If then she leaves this ruined tower, and goes
With buoyant heart unto her princely home—
Wearing gay smiles when her sad weeds are cast,
I will believe her false—and plunge
My dagger deep in her treacherous bosom—
But hark! what step intrudes——

[Lady Isabella *appears at a distance.*

[*Aside.*] 'Tis she, my Isabella ; down my heart,
Cease thy tumultous throbs ; let me retire.
[*Retires behind a rock.*
I dare not speak—scarce dare I gaze
Upon her wondrous beauty. Oh ! my love—
Far dearer now than when in youth I won thee !
Wert thou but true !—Oh, God ! oh, God !
Cast far from me that maddening thought !
Give back the freshness of my youthful heart,
Ere that false woman ruined every hope,
And taught me fell revenge as Heaven's best gift !
She speaketh ;—no, it is the moaning wind.
[Isabella *enters the castle.*
So quickly gone. My day's bright sun hath faded ;
Night comes apace. On, on, now, to my exile,
Beneath yon range of wave-worn rocks.

SCENE III.—*Room in the Tower.*

LADY ISABELLA.

L. Isabel. Three years have passed since my imprisonment.
Oh, weary hours, with nought to make their lapse

But my sad tears ; yet, with a woman's constancy,
I love the cruel heart that thus
Could bid me linger far, far from each fond tie.
My father, where art thou ? Who now will cheer
Thy sinking heart, when wintry age creeps on ?
With tender care watch thy slow faltering steps,—
And when that hour of mortal pain draws nigh—
As with deep groan the lingering soul springs
forth,
On its eternal flight,—who then will close thine
aged eyes
And weep above thy dear remains ?—[*Weeps.*

Enter AMELIA.

Ame. Dear lady, weep not so ;
There may be happy hours in store for thee ;
E'en now thy page from Dresden hath returned,
With messages and pacquet from thy friends.
Shall I admit him ?

L. Isabel. Do so, Amelia. [*Exit* AMELIA.
Alas, my heart speaks not of hope,

But some great woe weighs, with presentiment,
My senses down.

Enter AMELIA *and* Page.

Speak, boy, what says my father?
Ah! tears! he's dead! My heart
Forboded this.

Page. No, lady, no:
My lord the Duke is well.
He greets you kindly, and thus bade me say:—
With all good speed bid her to hurry on,
Her father sighs once more to bless his daughter.
This letter, lady, vouches for my truth—
This pacquet and this well known signet ring.

[LADY ISABELLA *takes the ring.*

L. Isabel. [*rapturously.*] My husband's ring!
Oh! happy fate! He has at length relented:
This letter will explain.

[Reads.] *Farewell; I died blessing my injured wife—*

[LADY ISABELLA *faints*—AMELIA *goes to her assistance.*

Ame. [*To* Page.] Quick, quick, some water—
Throw the casement open.
Alas, what aileth thee, dear lady ?
[*To* Page.] Hast thou brought tidings of evil import.

Page. Our noble master's dead,
And much I fear,
Our lady will not long survive him.

Ame. My lady's but a woman, after all—
Although a most discreet and virtuous one.—
She hath known much of sorrow, yet lived on ;
And this new grief but wears another form.
[*To* Page.] See, she revives, bring yonder goblet.
Drink, my sweet lady, 'twill restore thy strength.

L. Isabel. Cease, good Amelia,
I am well, quite well.
Leave me to my own thoughts.

[*Exit* Amelia *and* Page.

Gone ! the last hope that had sustained my spirit !
The stream flows on, though winter shred
The loveliest blossom that o'erhung its banks :
Thus wills the Almighty—good and merciful.
Forgive me, Heaven ! teach me to bow my heart
Unto the will of the All-wise Disposer.

Once more I will endeavor to peruse
This sad memorial.
[*Reads, interrupted by tears.*] My husband!
Would I had died for thee—and, dying, proved
My innocence;—but thus to leave me.—
Death! how terrible thou art,
Embittered by the thought of treachery.

Enter AMELIA.

Ame. My lady, did'st thou call?
L. Isabel. No, good Amelia;
But come hither to me.
It was his wish—my lord's last wish—
That I should choose my future residence
Where it may please me.
My choice is made; and here I will remain,
Nursing his loved remembrance, and my grief,
With such a churlish care, that none shall know
A widowed bosom dwells within these walls.
My honored father—I must e'en deceive him,
Lest, with a cruel kindness, he should call me
To the vain pomps I covet not.

But if within a convent's sacred walls
He deems I seek a refuge from my woes,
'Twill be a sanctuary which not e'en
A parent's love would tear me from.
Take thou this casket, which contains
Deeds of importance ; give it to my page,
And let him bear it to the Duke, my father.

[*Exit* AMELIA—LADY ISABELLA *leans on her couch, her face covered by her hands*—AMELIA *returns.*

And now, Amelia, can'st thou here remain,
Lonely and sad, to watch thy fading mistress ?

Ame. Dear lady, speak not thus :
Rememberest thou the tale thy mother told,
When here, upon this now deserted spot,
A happy family dwelt ;
And near a fisherman had reared his hut,
And earned a humble living by the sea ;
Which one dread night threw him a mangled corse
Upon the rocky shore. Two lived to mourn him :
One, a wretched wife ; the other, a young child
That knew not death, but played

With the long tangled locks that hung about it's
father.
Then came thy gentle mother, Lady Anne,
And snatched the babe from its sad play,
And bore it unto the castle, with its maniac
mother.
Lady, I am that child, and owe a debt
That time can never pay.

L. Isabel. Here, then, we will remain,
And dwell in solitude ;
This ruined home is the most fitting bower
For my wrecked heart. [*Exeunt.*

ACT II.

SCENE I.—*Mountain Scenery—A Hut.*

Banditti *disguised as Mountaineers.*

1st. Moun. Still absent!
Where roves the bold and gallant heart
That oft hath led us on to some rich spoil?
Rememberest thou the castle that we sacked,

The trembling band of women, whose shrill screams
Still seem to pierce mine ear?

2d. Moun. Well;
And our captain bade us lead them gently
Unto a neighboring hamlet—with strict command
To carry them in safety—bidding us remember
He warr'd not with young babes and trembling women.
Where roves he now? Angling for some fair fish,
And sparkling like a dolphin, when it glares
Beneath a sunny ray?

1st Moun. Beware; let us not forget we're mountaineers;
Join in the revel and the dance
With these wild mountain girls.—

Enter Peasant girls.

Hark! what sounds are these?
Heard ye not distant shouts?

Madeline. It is a band of soldiers on the search for the bold robber, who but late escaped from prison by a desperate attempt upon his keeper's life. He fled, it was supposed, to this wild spot.

2d Moun. A robber, said'st thou?

Mad. Where wert thou bred not to have heard of that famed robber chief? Where are your eyes—your ears? A mountaineer! good faith, I doubt thee much.

2d Moun. I was bred, my pretty Madeline, far from the spot where sparkle thy bright eyes. My ears are here open to list to thy speech; my mouth not too far off to answer thee.

[*Attempts to salute her.*

Mad. Stand off, my friend; your lips are eloquent, but my rejoinder may apply more strikingly. I doubt no more.

2d. Moun. Stay but a moment, gentle Madeline, I have much to say that may not be said as well on another day.

Mad. Say on.

2d Moun. Hast thou e'er loved? Of all thy friends, hast thou found one to whisper in thine ear how fair thou art?

Mad. Loved! oh, yes; most certainly I've loved. I love my mother—love my little dog—my last new ribbon and my scarlet boddice;—and as to flatterers, my dog fawns on me and my mother says I am her pretty Madeline; but, most of all, I love—

2d. Moun. Oh! speak.

Mad. I love my own dear will. Ha, ha, ha!

2d Moun. Well; thy dear Will am I. Is it not so?

Mad. Hush! hush! you weary me, go hence; here comes my mother with food and drink; refresh yourselves, then will we to the dance.

[*They sit down and take refreshments.*

Enter Soldiers.

Captain. In time to share your feast my pretty girl? Will you not welcome us with your sweet smiles?

Mad. [*curtseying.*] Welcome to our poor fare.

[*At this moment the* Outlaw *is seen cautiously descending the mountain at the back of the hut—the* Captain *catches a glimpse of him.*

Capt. Forward! my men. Now, by my halidame, there starts our game; the hunt is up;—seize, seize him instantly!

[Mountaineers *gently interpose.*

Capt. [*To* Moun.] Stand back, my friends; see you not the robber whom we seek? [*Mountaineers remain silent.*] Stand back or we will force you from your post.—On then, my men, the sturdy knaves abet him.

[Mountaineers *draw weapons from beneath their dress.*

1*st Moun.* We move not at thy proud request. Free men are we, that hold not to the slavish laws of citizens, but succor the oppressed.

Capt. Down, down with them my men!

[Helvitio *joins the* Mountaineers—*a Skirmish* —Soldiers *disarmed.*

Hel. [*To* Capt.] Rise, my brave foe, nor scorn
To take thy life a gift from outlawed hands.
For the space of three short hours,
Thou and thy men are captives;
That time elapsed, thou'rt free to seek again thy victor.

[*To* Moun.] My friends, we'll meet again,
Then will I thank you; now,
Each moment counts a death stroke to my life.

[*Exit.*

Capt. [*To* Moun.] Thou shalt repent thy most audacious conduct, and the authorities shall look into this wild seditious rising.

1*st Moun.* See'st thou that bird on yonder lofy tree?
Seek it and win it to obey thy will;
Or chain the wolf and bid it fawn on thee;—
These thou may'st do ere bend our hearts to cringe.
Thou art a captive and a captive's part is silence.

Enter MADELINE.

Mad. Have they all gone—that dreadful looking robber? Oh, oh! I am so frightened. You wicked man, how could you fight? Are any killed.

[*Sees the* Soldiers—*Screams.*

2*d Moun.* No, no, you silly girl, they are not

dead. What frightens you? Call out your laughing friends.

Come let us laugh, dance, sing, and joke and play,
Thus pass our time, joy comes not every day.

Mad. Dance! no, by my faith, I cannot. See how I tremble.

2d Moun. Come, come; take each a partner for the dance.

[*Dance—Stop to refresh themselves.*

Cap. Are we at liberty? The time hath past

Moun. Away, ye are free.

[*Exit* Soldiers—Mountaineers *about departing.*

Mad. Must you go? Well, well, I'll wait awhile for your return, ere I attempt to wed; a dozen hours perhaps: [*Goes to the door of the hut.*] Say, mother; shall I wait that age for our brave guest?

Old Woman. [*Comes forward.*] Aye, aye, child, I waited long enough for your old father; heaven rest his soul.

Mad. Well, then, good friend, I'll promise you, and like some ancient pagan, prize a brazen image.

2*l Moun.* Sweet Madeline, I swear the brass shall be well gilded ere I bring it back to my young worshipper. [*Exeunt* Mountaineers.

Mad. Come, mother, let us work, or else I'll weep—my heart's so heavy.

Old Woman. Poor child, you make me think of my young days. Come, scour away, and then we'll to our spinning.

SCENE II.—*Distant mountains*—Soldiers *descending—the Shore—a small Fishing Boat sheltered under a shelving rock.*

Enter HELVITIO.

Hel. Thus far I've fled, but now
My wearied limbs refuse to bear me;
Would I could see some friendly shallop near,
To aid me in escaping from my foes.
Hah! does my sight deceive me?
There is one close moored near yonder rock.—
Off, off my bark, thou bearest an outlawed freight.
[*Looses the boat.*

My gallant band, your chief from bondage freed,
Hastes to rejoin you ;
But first redeem my pledge to that base churl,
Who, with his shaking fingers, loosed my chains,
And bade me send a heavy ransom for it.
My sister, 'tis reported, is immured
Near this wild spot ;—
I'll hasten now to seek her ;
Oft she hath relieved my hard necessities ;
Praying me, with tears, to turn from my wild course.
But for her strict command, this trusty dagger
Would, ere this, have pierced her tyrant husband's heart.
I go to seek her.

[*Jumps into the boat.—Exit between rocks.*

Enter Soldiers.

Capt. Thus far, my comrades, fled the bandit chief.—
Six thousand marks are set upon his head—
A noble bounty for the border wolf ;

Would that it now were hanging to my belt,
And that rich sum beneath it.
The game is worth the toil;
Disperse, and hunt the wolf from out his den,—
He must have earthed him here.

[Captain *reclines on the rocks.—Exit* Soldiers *in all directions.*

What if the wolf should pounce upon me now?
I must be watchful; yet my laggard eyelids
Warn me to court repose.
Well, come what will, I'll sleep.

[*Sleeps.* Soldiers *seen at a distance scouring the country.*

[*Wakes startled.*] Upon my life, I thought his hand was on me!
Sleep, thou hast played strange pranks within my brain.
It is not pleasant to be taken prisoner,
Even in slumber. What, ho! my men!
Methinks I lack'd discretion
In letting all depart.

[Soldiers *seen returning.*

1st Soldier. Captain, we have scoured the country and have found no traces yet of the bold outlaw.

Cap. No signs, thou said'st?

1st Sol. None; sterile rocks alone have met
our view.
The night is falling, and a murky one 'twill be
In this wild place.
Bivouack we here, most noble captain?

Cap. No; on to yonder distantra nge;
There, by a mouldering cross
Which marks the grave of some poor traveller,
Stands a holy convent:
Shelter and food to all, unasked, are given.
On, comrades, on! I am no salt sea-bird
To build my nest on such a crag as this.
At dawn, to-morrow, we'll renew our search.

[*Exeunt* Soldiers.

SCENE III.—*View of the castle.*

OSCAR *concealed behind a rock.*

Enter HELVITIO *and* LADY ISABELLA.

Hel. Sweet sister, how can I repay thy love
To one outlawed from all his fellow nobles—
Alien from home and to his country's laws?—
Nay; seek not thus to change my roving life;
It suits my wild and savage temper best.
One kiss, sweet one: thou'lt seek our father's halls,
And cheer the old man with thy gentle presence.
We'll meet again this eve;
Have all prepared to meet thy brother's wishes.
[*Exeunt.*

Enter OSCAR.

Oscar, [*soliloquizing.*] Now, traitress,
Can I prove thee false at last;
And to thy fond and doting lord I'll fly
With these most cheering tidings.
Revenge is sweet, and now I've won its taste.

Did'st thou, fond fool, think to reject my suit,
And live unscathed? This to thy lord I'll say :—
At eve the Lady Isabella meets her paramour;
With tears and sobs this morning I saw them parting,
And weeping on his shoulder, thus she said:
When night her sober mantle throws around
I'll meet thee on this spot——

Enter AMELIA.

Ame. [*Suddenly intercepts* Os.] Who art thou,
That, with slow and stealthy step,
Art stealing round Malvino's lonely tower?

Oscar. A way-worn traveller, gentle dame,
Who seeks a shelter from the coming storm.

Ame. Pursue the path that lieth straight before thee;—
Soon will St. Hilda's convent meet thine eye—
There may'st thou shelter thee.—
The bandit, 'tis reported, are abroad;
Their chief, the far-famed robber of the Rhine,
Once more is free.
Heaven shield thee on thy way. [*Going.*

Oscar. Stay but a moment; who art thou?
Speak dame; thou hast a goodly presence,
And thy speech breathes of a gentle nature.

Ame. Here in thine ear I'll whisper it.——

Oscar. [*Starts.*] Hah!

Ame. Away, thou'rt safe; but hasten I entreat thee.
E'en now I see their glittering weapons gleam
With fitful lustre, as each vivid flash
From the dark clouds glance o'er them.

[*Exit* OSCAR.

Poor fool, thou flee'st as if a band of robbers were close upon thine heels; and thus I took the high and mighty title of bandit's bride to fright thee from thy purpose. Now go I to the Lady Isabel. I will describe this loitering knave's apparel—his figure—speech. She may, perhaps, unravel this seeming mystery. He looked not like a traveller.

[*Exit.*

SCENE IV—*A room in the castle.*

LADY ISABELLA *conversing with* AMELIA.

L. Isabel. Thou hast described that most deceitful friend. Well, my Amelia, when, at our Prince's court, I met his gaze, he did enquire my wealth and parentage—then sought my hand. His sordid suit rejected, with ill-disguised disdain, he vowed revenge. Alas! I tremble when I think of it; he was Alberto's friend; and, when betrothed to my lamented lord, I met this Oscar, he feigned a deep repentance. I believed and trusted him; that faith hath placed me here. 'Twas him abused my once kind husband's ear, with tales of my untruth; and urged him on, 'till, wrought almost to madness, he threw me from him. On that very night, beneath my casement, came my poor Helvitio. I saw him, as in pensive mood I leant, thinking of my lord's anger. I knew him instantly—my poor, poor brother! He came to hear some tidings of our father. My lord overheard our last few words, and seizing me with furious gesture, held his dagger to my bosom; then Oscar tore him from me and thus said :— *'Twere poor revenge to murder her, my friend ; a lingering life of close imprisonment will cure the lady's fancies.* That same night I was immured here. I fear him, good Amelia; haste to my brother's lurking place, and bring him tidings of coming danger; I will keep watch at yonder casement.

[*Exit* AMELIA. LADY ISABELLA *advances to the window.*

In yonder sky the heavy clouds
Are driven before the conquering wind;
And each bright star comes trembling into sight,
Fair as when first I gazed upon their light;
But the dark clouds of sorrow that o'ershade
My wearied soul—oh! never can they flee,
Since the bright sun of my existence set!

Enter AMELIA.

Ame. Thy brother says, dear lady, fear not for him; he will be with you in one moment's time. Hark! 'tis his step.

Enter HELVITIO.

L. Isabel. Welcome, my dear, dear brother!
But not a moment may'st thou stay with me;
I fear that spies are lurking near this spot.
My jewels I have here collected for you—
No other treasures hath your Isabella.

Hel. E'en keep them then to deck thy pretty self.—
Nay, I'll not rob thee, love.

L. Isabel. Stay, stay, Helvitio.
My father holds my rich domain for me;
And if thou could'st but find some trusty hand
To bear this little billet to him safely,
It will procure the sum thou dost require.
But, oh! dear brother! think on thy wild life.

[HELVITIO *takes the letter.*

Hel. My prison'd bird, thou singest very sweetly,—
Yet may I not list to thy mournful song.
Farewell, and seek a gay and gilded cage
Ere some wild prowler of the desert catch thee.

[*Exit* HELVITIO

SCENE V.—*A cave.*

OSCAR *and* ALBERTO *in conversation.*

Alber. This eve, thou said'st?
Oscar. Ay, ay, this very eve.
The storm is hush'd—all nature is combined
To give his love a hearing!
See how that star twinkles, as if it winked to us and said—
My friends, I see it all, but keep a lover's secret.
Thy wife is passing fair, my lord,—
Accomplished in all that doth become
A noble lady well; but she lacks discretion:
That rare costly gift hath been withheld
So fair a casket. Pity 'tis, indeed,
It holds not the rich gem.
Know you her lover? He wears a manly brow,
Embrown'd by foreign sun's; a bold demeanour;
Eye that hath the softness of the dove,
With the brave eagle's glance.
Alber. Enough; or I shall think thee some poor trader,
Vaunting thy goods.

Oscar. My friend, I pity thee; in truth I do.
Thou art an injured man.
Can I behold thee thrown upon this rocky floor—
Thy rival basking in thy wife's sweet smiles—
Nor wish a dire revenge?

Alber. Oscar, beware! thou call'st up a devil!

Oscar. Well! then we shall be three to one,
With thy ally to aid us!

Alber. Madman, desist!
My whirling brain's on fire, [*Musing.*]
To plunge my dagger deep, deep into her bosom!
No! 'twere too merciful! Her paramour,
Bathed in his blood, must meet her eye;
Then will I smile, and bid her kiss the lips
That made her play the wanton, ere I plunge
Her soul into perdition, there to meet him!
[*To* OSCAR.] I am resolved; on to the castle.
[*Exeunt.*

SCENE VI.—*The castle.*

OSCAR *and* ALBERTO *concealed near it.*

Alber. This is the place! Thou see'st I'm very calm.

Oscar. I do, my friend ;
Such calms too oft forbode a coming tempest.
Hah ! what heard'st thou 'neath that open casement ?

Alber. Naught ; naught but words ;
My lady's gay to-night.
I'll climb the broken wall and list awhile.
[*Climbs up. Decends rapidly.*
Let us begone !

Oscar. Alberto ! art thou mad ?
'Tis now the very hour——

Alber. Not now, not now !
I cannot watch them now !
Hark ! hear'st thou not her voice again ?
She prays for me ! for me—her lost lamented husband !
I do believe thee false, most false, Lord Oscar !
'Tis said thou wert an oft-rejected suitor.
Speak, man or devil !

Oscar. This to me !
But I forgive you, my much injured friend.
Let us away ; perhaps mine eyes deceived me :—

It might have been the Lady Isabel and her attendant.
I pray you pardon me for my too jealous love,
And look upon thy friend with kinder eyes.

Alberto. [*impatiently.*] E'en as you will.
[*Exeunt.*

SCENE VII.—*Morning.*

Enter HELVITIO *and* Banditti.

Hel. Here we'll await them.
See, the dawn is breaking; yon mountain top
Is tinged with the first smile of the fair sun;
All nature springs to greet it.
Think ye, my friends, the pallid slave
Who sinks, enervate, on his soft and silken couch,
Feels the wild joy that thrills through all our frames?
Give me the morning air—the midnight revel—
The toil—the tumult—and the battle strife,—
A quiet grave and most unquiet life!
Hark! now I hear the rocky pathway echo
With armed heels. Back; and, concealed

Each near some friendly rock, remain
Until the foe advance to seize me:
Then, on to the rescue!

[*Band conceal themselves.*—HELVITIO *folds his arms.*

Enter Soldiers.

Capt. Said I not so?
There stands the bandit chief, absorbed in reverie:
Advance and seize him!

[Soldiers *advance*—Robbers *start forward—a skirmish*—Soldiers *beaten off, pursued over the rocks by the* Banditti.—*Scene closes.*

ACT III.

SCENE I.—*Apartment in a palace in Dresden.*

DUKE MALVINO *reclining on a sofa.*

Enter Page, *and kneeling presents a letter.*

Page. Most noble duke; a wild and savage man,

With garments all disorder'd, as if with travel,
Pray'd at the porch to gain a quick admittance;
And being denied, produced this dust-soil'd billit,
And bade us, by the love we bore his daughter,
To place it safe within the Duke's own hand.

Duke. [*Takes the letter.*] My Isabella!
My poor, wretched child, it is thine hand;
Oh! would thou wert with thy old father.

[Reads.] *Six thousand marks*——

Ah! perchance to endow a convent.

[*To* Page.] Bid my steward give six thousand marks,
With quick dispatch, unto the messenger.

[*Exit* Page.

My child, could'st thou not serve thy God as well
In comforting thy lone and aged parent?
My son an outlaw; daughter thus immured,
Within a convent's cold and cheerless walls.
Oh! what are wealth and rank but glittering toys,
Without one child to bid my heart rejoice!

Enter Page.

Page. My lord, the money hath been paid.
Duke. 'Tis well.
Page. Pardon me, my lord, for speaking;
But it is said the famous Robber of the Rhine,
But lately captured, hath been brought, in chains,
To wait thy judgment.
Duke. Alas! alas! the penalty is great of worldly power:—
Must I condemn this man to death?
Take the bright cup of life from his parched lips,
And make his wife a widow, and his orphans
A bye-word and a stain upon the earth?
It must be so! Would that my aged head
Was laid in peace beneath the sheltering marble;
There are but few to weep for me,
And those—alas! I weep for them.

SCENE II.—*Street in Dresden.*

Enter Citizens.

1st Citizen. So the noted robber's safe at last?
2nd Cit. Thinkest thou he will be hung?

1st Cit. Aye if he has a neck to hold the rope,
His fate is certain. To-day, at twelve o'clock,
His pranks are ended.

2nd Cit. Hark! 'tis the time;
I hear the coming crowd. Stand back
And let us both look on the show.

Enter Crowd, Soldiers, *&c.*

Oscar *with a rope round his neck.*

1st Cit. A villanous countenance!

2nd Cit. A most bloody one!

1st Cit. So wags the world! One day at liberty,
The next, caught like an ape, with noose about the neck.
Heaven! should we prove so tight a neck cloth——

2nd Cit. Thou'rt safe, my friend;
Heaven, in forming thee, forgot the neck.
Thou'lt live to good old age
If apoplexy does not catch thee napping.

1st Cit. Truly, friend, you need not mock my goodly size,

When thou an apt resemblance art of some lean dog,
Snarling and fighting over a marrow bone.

2nd Cit. Truce, a truce. Come, let us to the show,
A man is not hung every day.

[*Exeunt.*

SCENE III.—*Market-place.*

DUKE *seated on a temporary throne*—OSCAR, *the supposed* Robber *petitioning.*

Oscar. Your highness, listen but one moment to me:
My name is Oscar;—know ye not Alberto's friend?
'Tis but a week since I have parted from him.
I am an innocent and injured man;
Imprison'd, manacl'd, and led to judgment:
For what offence, most mighty Duke?
Look I so like a robber, that, wand'ring
By a rude and rugged cliff that o'erhung the sea,
I should be seized for that famed robber who so oft

Hath struck terror into the bosom of the brave?
Whose name, a bug-bear with which mothers
Fright their babes to slumber?
Look at me once again; I am lord Oscar!
Perhaps some here may know me.—
Are there none, none of my towns-men present?
I do beseech thee to release me, Duke.

Duke. Away, most wretched man!
Thou dost abuse mine ear with thy false tale:
The lord Alberto's dead!
Off to his doom with the vile slave!

[OSCAR *is hurried off.*

SCENE IV.—*View of the Castle.*

Enter LADY ISABELLA *and* HELVITIO.

Lady Isabella. What madness prompted thee,
Helvitio, to this spot?
I tremble, lest the much-abused law
Should seize thee in thy sister's arms.

Helvitio. No, trembler, no: Helvitio's safe!
The Bandit chief hath met at last his doom.—

Thou doubt'st me? Truly thou may'st well,
When a corporeal form I stand before thee!
I will unravel this strange mystery:—
A man was found, lurking about the spot,
Where I was said to hide,—
And, seized by those who sought my life,
They gave to him a most exalted fate:—
He died upon a lofty scaffolding.—
Nay, droop not, Isabella! I could not save!
I heard the tale hours after his sad fate.
Rouse thee, dear one! speak, speak to thine own
brother!

[HELVITIO *supports his Sister.*

L. Isabel. [*faintly.*] It was lord Oscar!

Enter ALBERTO, *disguised as a Hermit.*

Alber. [*furious with passion.*] Die!

[*Stabs* LADY ISABELLA.—HELVETIO *too late to arrest the stroke, springs upon* ALBERTO. LADY ISABELLA *for a moment revives and sees her brother in danger.*

L. Isabel. My brother! save thee! oh, fly!

Alber. Her brother! [*Drops the dagger.*]

Helv. Murderer! defend thyself!
Helvitio seeks not an assassin's blood, but in an open strife!
Coward! dost thou refuse? Thus, then!—

Alber. Hold, hold! I am thy sister's husband!
[*Tears off his disguise.*
[*To the body of* LADY ISABELLA.] Sweet saint!
Thus I revenge thee!
[*Springs from the rock.*

Enter AMELIA.

My lady, what now? My gentle lady!
Great Heaven! why lies she thus?—blood, blood!
Helvetio, is this thy work? Oh, no; forgive me.
[*Weeps.*

Helv. Amelia, thy lov'd mistress lies there dead!
Aye! murdered by her husband!
The deed accomplished, in maniac mood
He sprang o'er yonder rock ere I could save him,
Or revenge her death!

'Twas said he went abroad and there had died:
'Twas false—most false;—he had returned,
Deceived my sister with his feigned death,
And loitered here [*to corpse*] to prove thee false.
Sweet saint! his jealous madness urged him on to this.

Ame. [*weeping.*] Oh! my lord Helvetio! by this dear one,
Whose blood cries up to warn thee,
Fly to thy father! for his mercy sue:
He hath the power--the will to pardon thee.
In the proud heir of thy most princely house
What man can recognize the outlaw'd boy
Who plunged his dagger in a kindred's bosom?

Hel. True, true, Amelia;
To meet my doom or pardon I go.
Let my poor Isabella be the sad partner
Of my weary journey.

SCENE V.—*Palace in Dresden—an apartment.*

DUKE, Attendants.

Duke. What means this tumult in my peaceful halls?

Out, knaves, and see what turbulent uproar
Thus breaks upon my quiet.

[*Exeunt* Attendants.

Enter PAGE.

Page. [*sadly.*] Your highness, be prepared;
There are evil tidings; grief is at your door.
My noble master be prepared to hear them.

Duke. Boy, grief is my inmate!
Years have rolled on, and yet she loiters.
Think ye a greater evil can befal a wretched father,
Who for years hath mourned an absent child,—
A lov'd but outlaw'd son?
Speak on, nor fear, though death were in thy tidings.

Page. The lady Isabella is sick to death:
She sends you tidings of her hopeless illness.

Duke. Dying! haste—haste!
My horses—bring them quickly hither!
I'll on to thee, my poor deserted child!
Why stand ye loit'ring? death may meet mine eyes!—

Away—away! this is no time for tears!

Page. Too late, I fear, great Duke;
My lady is dead.

[DUKE *sinks into his chair.*

Duke. My child! my child!

Page. Your highness, pardon me;
Her sole attendant waits below—
The Lady Isabella's trusted servant, dame Amelia.

Duke. Bring her to me, we'll mourn together.

Exit Page.—DUKE *remains silent in deep grief.*

Enter AMELIA.

Ame. Great Duke, thus far I've travel'd
With a grief that weighs my sinking spirit to the earth;
You mourn a child, and I a cherished mistress;
One who to me was child, protectress, friend.
Sole relic of that much abused saint,
Whom, I trust, receives the just reward
Of her sad trials here,
Upon thy bounty now I throw myself.

Duke. Receive it good Amelia;
All my possessions were too poor a recompence
For thy tried service.

Ame. Your highness, I thank you humbly.
One request my gentle mistress made in her last sickness:—
"Bear me," she said, "when dead, unto my father's halls,
That one prized tear may fall upon my corpse,
And hallow it. Oh! bear me to my father!"
I have complied, most faithfully, my lord;
Her saintly form rests in thy tapestried chamber.

Duke. Oh, Heaven! I thank thee for this sad, sad blessing!
My good Amelia, give me thine arm;
Bring me to my child! [*Exeunt.*

SCENE VI.—*A small Room in the Ducal Palace.*

HELVITIO *alone.—Enter* AMELIA.

Hel. How bears my father this said stroke, Amelia?

Sunk he beneath the blow?
Alas! I fear his aged heart is broken.

Ame. Age hath no heart to break; yet, in his countenance,
I saw a calm so desolate, my lord Helvetio,
The most clam'rous grief were nought to it.

Hel. Can I then break upon his solitude—
Disturbing, with new grief, his mourning soul?
No, no; I may not—dare not: I will remain concealed
'Till time hath given balm to his sad heart.
Go thou, Amelia, comfort my old father.

Ame. I go, my lord;
Should'st thou have need of ought, touch this small bell;
'Twill bring one quickly to thee who may be trusted. [*Exit Amelia.*

Hel. Once more an inmate in my father's halls!
How throbs my breast with an unknown tumult!
How oft I've passed my childish days
In roving through these wide halls;

Or, in this same apartment, sitting and list'ning to my nurse's tales,
With wondering ears and open mouth'd surprise
At each wild legend.
Seems it so long since that gay childish era?
Alas! the boy has merged into the man,
Grown old in recklessness and sin,—
Hah! who disturbs me? is it thou, Amelia?

Enter AMELIA, *agitated.*

Ame. My lord, my lord! haste, haste!
Your dying father calls on his son, hopeless of seeing him!
Grief hath preyed heavily on his aged heart;
I found him senseless by my lady's corpse;
Assistance came at my shrill screams;
We bore him to his chamber,
Called in the leech, who shook his head and sighing,
Took his station aside his highness' bed.
All hope is o'er; thy father, weeping, calls upon his child,

His Isabella; then bids his servants ride express
For his long exiled son.

Hel. Lead on, Amelia; exiled though I was by my stern father,—
Brutus like condemning his only son,—
Yet my long exile o'er even justice cannot claim again a victim:
My heart yearn's for my aged parent's blessing.

[*Exeunt.*

SCENE VII.—*Ducal apartments.*

DUKE, *reclining cn a bed*—Physician, Attendants.

Enter AMELIA *and* HELVITIO.

Duke. More would I say, but my lungs are wasted,
Sinking 'neath unwonted efforts.
If my son returns, give true allegiance to my rightful heir:
My blessing rests upon him.

[HELVITIO *springs to the bed.*

Hel. My father!

Duke. Who calls? what voice is that?
My eyes are dim, yet sounded it most wondrously
like his;—
My son! my son!

Hel. Oh! pardon me, my father!
Alas, how cold thy hand strikes to my heart!
Live, live! oh, live! that I may show the world
How changed Helvitio is!

Duke. My son, where art thou?
Nearer! still more near!—let me feel your hand!
Bless you! stay, go not yet.—
I cannot see thee!—throw back the hangings!—
Too late! too late! [*Pauses.*]
Night creeps apace: my son, reign over my peace-
ful subjects.
Farewell! I go to meet thine angel sister! [*Dies.*

END OF THE OUTLAW.

MISCELLANEOUS POEMS.

MISCELLANEOUS POEMS.

CAN THE VOICE DIE?

A vision came in the starry night,
  When I in slumber lay—
The slumber free from earthly blight
  When the soul hath purer sway.

On the verge of the spirit world I stood,
  'Mid the holy and the pure;
Around me, light in a living flood,
  Whose blaze I could scarce endure.

I saw the bright form of seraphim,
  As I knelt with the forgiven,
And sang the ever-enduring hymn—
  The praise of the God of heaven.

Yet my spirit was sad: alone, alone,
  I seemed in that happy sphere;
I pined for a lost familiar tone—
  A voice that on earth was dear.

Hark! a new gush of melody!
  Oh! glorious, glorious strain!
That voice—it rose cheerly and joyfully,
  Welcoming me again.

MEDORA'S SONG.

Ah! let me rest thus at thy side,
  As I was wont of yore,
And touch my Lyre, whose every chord
  Is filled with love's sweet lore;

And clasp thine hand within mine own—
  The hand I love to press,
And feel thou hast returned to me,
  In all thy faithfulness.

'Twas sad to raise my eyes alone,
  Unanswered by thine own,
To listen until sinking hope
  Had lost thy faintest tone.

To feel the magic of thy voice
  But come to me in dreams,
As rest the shadows of sweet flowers
  Upon the moon-lit streams.

That pleasant voice that speaks to me
  Of passion's fervent hour;
Hours which o'er life's worst darkness fling
  Affection's soothing power.

As morning hues upon the sea
  Seem blended with the sky,
From which it borrows all the tints
  That on its calm waves lie.

So blended seems my soul with thine,
  So borrow I sweet thought,
In gazing on those deep-soul'd eyes,
  So with love's mysteries fraught.

Then let me rest thus by thy side,
  And feel that thou art near,
For never, till we parted, love,
  Knew I thou wert so dear.

SONG.

I remember, I remember, though it seems to me
a dream,
Or a sunbeam, fleeting o'er the wave, that
brighten'd 'neath its beam.
Dost thou ask what I remember? 'twas a smile
from one I knew,
And a glance from a blue merry eye, and words
that seem'd so true.
Now I press my burning hand, to a brow that
throbs with pain,
Whilst mem'ry brings each kindly look and ac-
cent back again.

I was happy, I was happy then, in gazing on
his face—
Nor would I wish that time should e'er, those
words and looks efface;
For I feel, when in my weariness I sit and weep
alone,
That mem'ry is the only good I now may call
my own.

I remember, I remember, like sweet music soft
and low,
A voice that made my pulses thrill, and bade my
pale cheek glow;
And the words, the words then uttered (oh! could
they be but art?)
When death hath summon'd me away, thou'lt
find upon mine heart
We parted, yes, we parted, like a rudely wrenched
chain,
As if each broken link and clasp could ne'er unite
again.

They said that he was weary of a love that could
not change—
They told me that his fickle heart a trifle would
estrange;
And I spoke with bitter scornfulness, in words I
deeply rue,—
How could I think a heart like his could ever
prove untrue?

ON LISTENING TO THE MUSIC OF THE TELEGRAPHIC WIRES.

Viewless spirit! what melody divine
  In the 'mid air now swelleth?
Lost Pleid! is the heavenly harping thine?
  That sighing cadence of such sorrow telleth,
As if thou for thy star-gemmed crown did'st pine.

Swells the loud peal in a triumphal strain,
  Until the welkin ringeth.
Faintly, and mournfully it breathes again!
  Lost, lost! forever lost! Thou singeth
For earthly love, that bringeth nought but pain!

IMPROMTU
ON AN
ENGRAVING OF THE BETROTHED SPIRITS.

Hist! 'tis faint music swelleth on the air;
And, by the glow-worm light, a Pageant fair,
With myrtle chaplets 'mid their locks entwined,
Float softly by, like the sweet song of nightingales combined.

Spirits of the betrothed! freed from the thrall
Of the dull earth! Pure as ere woman's fall;
Their love all spiritual. With gentle smile,
Backwards they cast their eyes, and murmur, dear ones, yet awhile!

Glide on thou purely beautiful! thy forms
Float in mid ether—calm above the storms
Of thy heart's tempest; whilst, with streaming eyes,
Thy earth-bound lovers kneel, and mourn thy progress through the skies.

TO THE ABSENT.

Come to me, love; knowest thou the dew is falling,
And the pure star-light gleams o'er hill and dale?
Come, ere my lips are weary with their calling,
And the soft cheek thou lovest turneth pale.

Why dost thou linger? clouds are gathering round me,
But not the summer's gentle threatnings lour;
'Tis the heart's gloom, dearest, ere grief hath bound me
In his strong fetters;—come, and joy restore.

Call I in vain? my children, the young voices
  Join to your mother's! bid wild echo ring
With the loved name that still my heart rejoices,
  As in our love's first fair and joyous spring.

Would I could hear his steps, as music cheering
  To the lone watching heart—bid him draw near,
And from the brow, pale with love's anxious fearing,
  Kiss the deep sadness and starting tear!

Hark! 'tis his step! quick, quick, and haste to meet him!
  E'en through the darkness I can mark his gaze,
Hasten, my children! warmly, kindly greet him.
  Home safe! to heaven now give thy grateful praise.

THE LOVE OF OTHER DAYS.

(FROM THE GERMAN.)

It was the sunset hour, and richly fell the gleam,
In beauty blended o'er the earth, rose-hued and golden beam;

It played about a casement, an old man rested there,
But pallid were his aged lips, as was his whited hair.

Calm seemed the old man's slumber,—why drew they back in dread?
It was the calmness of the grave, the slumber of the dead.
We tremble at the warning, that tells us from the earth,
A spirit hath, in joyfulness, sprung to a holy birth!

Within his withered fingers, clasped with a dying hold,
There seemed a gem of beauty;—did the old man prize the gold?
Oh! shame on such base feeling! when they loos'd the stiffened hand,
A lovely pictur'd face was there, a dark and braided band.

Oh! love unchanged, unchangeable! time hath o'er thee no power,—

And pleasant was the old man's death, at sunset's
glowing hour!
Amidst the fields of memory, the sorrow's course
may run,
The sun of other days can shed light o'er the
closing one.

STANZAS.

"Tell me, Spirit of the Sea,
Why the ocean's murmur dwells,
Hidden in coils so cunningly,
In the breast of the couch-like shells?"

And the voice of the Spirit said:
"Hidden from me is the mystery
Of the ocean's mighty bed."

I asked the Spirit of the Flowers,
Why it closed each little bell
When the sun had left its bowers,
And the shades of evening fell.

And the Spirit answered me:
"Seek not to know—a higher power
Hath will'd it so should be."

I turned to the Zephyr near :—
  "Light Spirit, oh, tell me true,—
Whence came the wind you wafted here?
  Tell me, where will it wander to?"

And the voice of the Zephyr said :
  "I wander over the earth so fair,
By Creation's Law still led."

Then my soul was sad with awe,
  Of the solemn mysteries,
Of the Earth and Sky, and the Law
  That governed the mighty seas!

Then the Hidden Spirit spoke,
  Within my soul, of the Deity,
Who the bonds of chaos broke.

"Praise, praise to His holy power,
  Forever on earth be given!
Seek, mortal, ere thy parting hour,
  To know thy God in Heaven!

TO MARY.

Come, my sweet one, 'tis thy slumbering hour ;
With clasped hands bend humbly to that Power—
The Giver of all good, all joy to thee :
Who, my young child, can that kind influence be?

Mother, I look on the glowing sky,—
On the bright stream that bubbles and gushes by ;
On the earth, with its beautiful flowers and trees,
And I hear sweet music upon the breeze !
The birds have a voice of song and glee,
But the Power you speak off I cannot see !
Is He on earth, 'mid the flowers so sweet?
Mother, his foosteps may I meet,
And thank Him for all His love to me?
Oh ! mother, why look you so mournfully?

My gentle one :—when your young bird died,
Remember how sadly you sobb'd and cried?
When its notes were mute, nor answered your
glee,
Look'd you not then most mournfully?

With a mother's anxious grief I wept,
To think that, perhaps, while my lov'd one slept,
Her spirit might pass to that heaven above,
Where dwelleth in glory the Power of Love;
But not till you pass through the shades of death,
And I feel no more your gentle breath
On my cheek—soft, glowing and warm, my child,
And miss your sweet looks and accents mild,—
Not till then may you meet with that holy Power,
And I wept to think of our parting hour.

SONG.

There's a smile on thy lips, Mary,
Like the gleam from a sunny sky
On a mirror'd lake,
When its waters break
Into ripples, and dimple by.

There's a tear 'neath thy dropping lid,
Like the dew by a rose-leaf hid,
When the mid-day sun,
From all but that one,
The tears of the night-spirit chid.

Yet I trust not thy smile, my fair,
For the waters, when troubled, are
    Too rough for my skill,
    And a tear at will
A lady too often may bear.

Yet 'tis sweet, in the sunny beam,
To sail over some placid stream,—
    As away we glide
    On the sunny tide,
Of bowers of roses to dream.

A PENITENT'S ADDRESS TO THE MUSE.

And have I then forgotten thee, my spirit's early love,
Nor listened to thy gentle voice, soft breathing from above?
Forgive, forgive, sweet poesy,—thy truant lover hear,
And lend, to his repentant prayer, once more a lenient ear.

'Tis true I've bowed at many a shrine, and bent a willing knee,—
But the poet's soul, in each fair form, saw but a type of thee!
Awhile the beauteous picture traced, by Fancy's graceful hand,
Enthrall'd my senses, and I bowed to Love's supreme command.
Forgive, forgive thine erring one, the phrenzied dream is o'er!
Those lips that breathed of summer flowers, no voice of music bore,—
Those eyes that burned with passions light were false, I broke the spell!
How could I deem my spirit's love in such a form could dwell!
As soon upon the bounding wave, fair nature's gorgeous dress,
Of wreathed buds and fragrant plants, may spread in loveliness;
As the poet's soul, enthrall'd, forget its home, its heavenly birth,
And bow each glorious attribute to a mere child of earth!

LOVE, REASON, AND TRUTH.

"Where, oh where's the chain to fling,
One that will bind Cupid's wing?"
On the wings of the wandering breeze,
  Love joyed to float away,
Forgetting those who were ill at ease,
  While he was off at play.

Venus vowed that it should not last,—
  'Twas time that he went to school,
For his boyhood in ignorance had past,
  And he never had learn'd a rule.

She sprang in her chariot of blue,—
  (It was drawn by a turtle dove,)
Of a serious, sensible dame she knew,
  Who might teach a lesson to Love.

In tears Love came—he did not dare
  To refuse, but felt in a fret;
She wiped off his tears with her golden hair,
  And said, now be quiet my pet!

They soon alighted at Reason's gate,—
  Truth stood at the open door;

Come back ! cried Cupid ; 'tis not too late !
Oh ! Reason is such a bore.

And Truth hath a look, oh, mother dear,
That I never yet could brook ;
She chills me,—and Reason, too much I fear,
I never can learn her book !

So fretted and fumed the petted child,
As his mother turned to go ;—
She said : my boy is a little wild,
You had better hide his bow.

Alas, for Reason ! alas, for Truth !
Would we know what both befel ?
He hood-winked Reason, that artful youth,
And tumbled Truth in a well.

SONG.

Come, wreathe round my brow
Those pale, sweet flowers !
Were they not made for the festal hours,
When the cup, like a sparkling ruby glows,

And the rich red wine to the brim o'erflows,
And the heart, like a bird
From its thraldom free,
Flutters and carols so joyfully ?
Then twine round my forehead those fragrant flowers,
They were made, like young beauty, for festal hours.

Come, cheer up my fairest !
Each flowing curl
I will twine with a chaplet of snowy pearl ;
Not a gem 'mid their raven hue must shine,—
Thou would'st dim them, my Love, with those orbs of thine !
Nay ! shade not their beam
Mid the clear blue skies ;—
When the bright sun sinks the pale flower dies !
Then twine round my forehead those fragrant flowers,
They were made, like young beauty, for festal hours.

TO THE AUTHOR OF "A NEW READING OF OLD SONGS."

Dear Illustrator of old rhymes,
Thou mindest me of ancient times,
When you and I together
Roved, seeking butterflies and flowers—
Despising damp—forgetting hours—
With hearts light as a feather.

Now, we have toils and cares and troubles;
Yet, still, time finds us blowing bubbles,
And spreading nets and cages:
You read old songs another way,
And well and quaintly do you play
The gamut of mirth's pages.

I, though not blue, nor deeply read,
Have rashly dared the muse to wed,—
Forgetful of the penance:
An empty purse to those who've sung,
An attic, high as Haman hung:—
What care I for the menace!

My heart is light—my garret dry,
And something nice when friends are nigh ;
And you, my frolic brother,
Have added to my treasured store
Of pleasant thoughts an item more,
And helped me care to smother.

Thus let us while each idle hour,
Pluck here a fruit—cull there a flower,
Bid life new impulse borrow,
And innocently pass our time
Till called unto a happier clime,
That knows not care nor sorrow.

THE IMPATIENT.

Why stays he thus ? he would be here
If his love equalled mine ;—
Methinks, had I one fond caged dove,
I would not let it pine !

He comes no more to see me,—
(He called me his wild flower,)
I hear that winning sound no more,—
But, oh! I feel its power.

I'm weary with my watching—
Because I watch in vain;—
But woman's heart must suffer much
In solitude and pain.

What is it keeps him from me?
Oh! if my eyes are dim,
He might have known 'twas weariness,
In watching long for him.

And if my cheek has faded,
Kind words could make it bloom;
His voice could call my spirit back,
Though sinking to the tomb.

But now I'll weep no more—
Why should I weep in vain?
Oh! robe me in a garb of pride,
Deck me with jewel'd chain!

I'll seek, in halls of splendor,
Forgetfulness and Scorn;
The blood of my own haughty line,
Hath ill his falsehood borne.

The red-rose on my forehead,
Shall brightly bloom at eve;
Farewell, farewell, false love of mine,
No longer will I grieve.

Scarce had the maiden spoken,
When, springing to her side,
A manly form kneels at her feet,—
Oh! where was woman's pride?

"TO DIE IN SUMMER'S PRIDE, ALAS!

I am weary, I am weary, my frame is rack'd with pain,—
Upon my fever'd couch I lie—shall I e'er rise again?
My pulses throb thro' every vein,—faint, faint and sad my heart,
But the grievous agony of all, it is with thee to part.

From thee, beloved, to sever! oh, must I feel this grief?
Is there no healing balm, no hope of a relief?
Thy voice at midnight hour, thro' restless dreams I hear,—
How blest if that deep loving voice once more might meet mine ear.

I would not that thy memory should dwell on this sad hour!
No; think of me when pleasure calls each votary to her bower;—
In thine hours of mirth and gladness, when music floats around,
Think, then, thou hearest the lov'd one's voice in every gentle sound.

Cherish her memory fondly! oh! was she not to thee
A dream of joy, a being full of love and constancy?
Upon this earth, beloved, once—only once, we find
Soul meeting soul!—yet must we die! this bitter truth I find.

Now, fare thee well! my pulses are faint; before
my eyes
Shadowy forms are hovering, and misty clouds
arise;
Oh! could I clasp thine hand once more, and feel
thy sweet warm breath
Upon my cold and pallid lips, love then might
conquer death!

SONG.

"Hew! quoties fidem,
Mulatosque Deos flebit."—HORACE.

Bring me roses, red roses, to fling o'er my wine,
As I fling from my heart this false image of thine;
Their fragrance alone on my lips now may dwell;
I've broken the last tie, I've thrown off love's spell.
Ere the last leaf has faded, the last drop is shed,
Will the passion, once cherished, for ever have
fled.

I awake, as from sleeping the mariner springs
From his hammock, when loudly the storm o'er
him sings,
And the breakers are dashing white foam round
the prow
Of the vessel, that strikes, e'er sleep leaveth his
brow.
Ah! the waters that close o'er that lone seaman's
head,
Are calm, to the bosom whose last hope hath fled!

Yet bring me the wine-cup, let music breathe on;
Shall my cheek, for the lost smile of woman,
grow wan?
No! we'll part whilst the perfume of flowers floats
around;
And I'll drown thy false words in the harp's ring-
ing sound,—
As the famed bird of beauty that pines for its mate,
And mourns, in sweet numbers, its nest desolate!

TO R——

"If, in this world of breathing harm,
There lurk one universal charm,
'Tis the pure *kiss* of infant love."

I gaze on thee, my own fair child,
With thy graceful form and actions wild,—
(As you bound, like a fawn, on the grassy plain,
Stopping each moment to laugh again,)
With a throbbing breast as away you rove,
A heart so full of a mother's love!

Thy sunny smile and thy childish glee,
Come o'er my soul like sweet minstrelsy;
And I fly from the world's delusive bliss,
To lighten my heart with a sight like this!
Yes, my sweet one, thy faintest tone,
Is a blessed pledge,—I am not alone.

Can it be, that young heart should ever swell
With the pangs that too oft in my bosom dwell?
Must that fair young brow, and that beaming eye,
Be dimmed by the world, and the wearied sigh,

And in secret droop o'er the ruined hope,—
Fair child, must thou e'er with such sorrows cope?

Thou must, sweet one! too well I know
That sorrow's the portion of all below,
But we'll heed it not, for full soon, alas!
Will thy joyous moments of pleasure pass.
Then come, let us play in the sunny beam,
And not of the world of sorrow dream.

"WINTER, WITH SNOW-FLAKES ON HIS HOARY BROW."

The voice of the Frost-King is on the breeze:
He comes!—wo! wo! for the leafy trees!
They mourn, for his breath is scatt'ring the pride
Of their summer apparel on every side.
The Violet and Columbine both are dead,
And the Cardinal's gone from its marshy bed,—
The Willow is weeping above their tomb,
For the lost ones were fair in their summer bloom.

'Tis Winter ! dread Winter!—I know him now—
The snow-flakes are thick on his aching brow ;
He exults o'er the autumn, whose early death
Was caused by the cold from his icy breath.
Nay ! ring not thy sleigh-bells—I will not go !
Your sled may glide on,—I hate the snow.
You have swept all my trees of their glorious hues,
You have frozen the twilight's fragrant dews,
The locust and humming bird both are away—
The land is desolate !—why should I stay ?
Was it an echo, borne on the breeze,
As it murmured in sadness, thro' leafless trees ?
Was it that voiceless tone that said,
Stay !—And I answered, with whom ?—the dead ?
The dead ! their remembrance and grief may die,
As the flowers of the Summer forgotten lie ;
But the buried thoughts we had deemed at rest,
Burst from their secret tomb—the breast ;—
And they whisper, (those spirits of happier hours,)
Heed not the faded leaves and flowers !
Come with us to the lonely wood,
Nourish us fondly in solitude ;

Joy we may give, tho' we have no spell
To bring back the past ye have lov'd so well:
Stay! And hope brightened the wintry sky,
With so rosy a hue—that—could I deny?

VOICE OF THE THUNDER-CLOUD.

From my home, 'mid storms I spring,—
  Child of the summer day,—
O'er the wither'd buds I wildly fling
Dew, from the brush of my sable wing;
The birds, when I flee, leap forth and sing,
  As I rove o'er my trackless way.

Afar, o'er the sea I glide;
  The billows I unchain,
Till they lash the struggling vessel's side;
A wreck on the wave I see her ride!
Then, groaning, plunge in the foaming tide,
  Whilst I lighten with joy the main.

The Heaven's bright smile I veil,
  Each planet's sparkling gaze,—
With jealous care—'mid the sky I sail,
(By the wild winds borne, with moan and wail,)
I shadow the moon, now faint and pale,
  And my offspring—the lightning—plays.

I strike with a fiery dart,
  Ere they hear my dreaded tone,
The loved and the loving ; I could not part
The bands that were woven from heart to heart ;
But I knew they were free from the worlding's
    art,
  And 'twere worse to live alone.

Alas! alas! that I bear
  Such sorrow o'er the earth!
When I strive to lighten the thicken'd air,
And freshen the buds, with anxious care
My path is followed, and fell despair,
  Where I looked for joy and mirth.

But, tho' high my destiny,
  The chilling north-west blast

Comes sweeping o'er the ruffled sea,
The brown leaves are whirling from bush and tree,
The birds take wing and afar they flee,—
And I feel that my reign is past.

ON A VIOLET.

I placed thee on my breast, sweet flower;
There, thou did'st live thy little hour.
I pluck'd thee not from nature's bower—
But he—whom I love best,
Gave thee to me, with sunny smile,
One quiet moonlight night:
And though it seemeth a long while,
I cannot think that ought of guile
Could dim that smile's pure light.

I prized the gift, but oh! much more
The sun-bright smile his features wore:
Ah! if these happy days are o'er,
Still of that smile I'll dream.

In vision, it will come to bless,
When length'ning shadows fall;
And twilight, with her sombre dress
Stealeth around in loneliness,
'Twill shed a gleam o'er all.

—

————" Thence it came,
That she, whom all men prais'd, and whom myself,
Since I have lost, have lov'd, was in mine eye
The dust that did offend it."—SHAKSPEARE.

TO CORA.

By the memories deep and thrilling,
By each slumbering chord of joy,
By each fond hope of the future—
Hope's absence may destroy;
Return, my being's idol,
Whilst life's in each warm vein;
Return—return to love's true shrine,
I call thee back again.

Thou art the spirit of my dreams,
My being's very soul;
I think of thee till passion spurns
All reason—all control;
I'll hold thee yet the dearer
And strive with mingled art,
(Art taught by Love) to win again
That proud but gentle heart.

I have gloried in thy name, love,
I have trembled for thy weal,
The eloquence of those dear lips
Thro' every pulse I feel;
And when I list to others, and
They name thy treasured name,
Mingled with praises of thy worth,
Thy talents and thy fame.

My kindling brow, my blushing cheek,
My throbbing heart betray—
That o'er my bosom love hath won
A wild, unbounded sway.

Return then, my beloved,
  Whilst life throbs in each vein,
For death in life I suffer 'till
  Thou com'st to me again.

INVOCATION.

Stay, dear one, time may never bring
Another moment on his wing
  So rich with bliss :
See, 'mid the sun-lit Heavens on high
Hang blushing clouds, a canopy
  Whose shadows kiss
The trembling waves, that bound to meet
The sun's last glances, ere they fleet
  Like visioned hopes.
My own, my blest, mark how below
The field and woodlands brightly glow ;
  Kind nature opes
Her richest stores—'tis a fair scene,
And thou, of beauty art the queen,
  My lov'd, my dear !

Stay, nor like that bright orb depart—
Thine eyes are to my beating heart
  A sunny sphere—
Thou wilt not? cruel! fare thee well;
Heed not my tears that gushing swell!
  Far from my sight,
Go, go—I would not bid thee stay,
My life—my bliss thou bearest away,
  Good night—good night.

THE DESERTED WIFE.

I cannot sleep—I cannot rest,
  My weary heart is aching;
I watch the glowing of the West,
  I see the morning breaking.

And then, I long again for night—
  For night, and then for morning,
But ah! the smile that was my light
  Is turned to bitter scorning.

May Heaven preserve me in this hour,
And keep me e'er from madness
Uphold me with its strength'ning power
To bear this mortal sadness.

Hush! hush, my babe, thy little moan,
And closer to me nestle,
We now must struggle on alone
With worldly sorrows wrestle.

Alone, alone, my fatherless,
We'll stem life's troubled ocean—
Ah! woe is me! and sore distress!
And weary wild commotion.

For he, who welcomed thee, my child,
With smiles and fond caresses,
Another hath his love beguiled,
Another's lip he presses.

Hero.—"And here's another,
Writ in my cousin's hand, stolen from her pocket,
Containing her affection unto Benedick."—SHAKSPEARE.

TO ——

Yes, love me for myself alone,
And love me very truly !—
Ye all are apt to promise this,
When ye have loved but newly.

Remember that this cheek will fade—
Mine eyes lose all their brightness.
And the fairy foot, you flatter now,
In age—forget its lightness.

I plight thee here an honest heart,
A heart that feels sincerely—
I never thought I could have lov'd
As I do love thee—dearly.

Then trust me, as I've trusted thee,
And with a love as real ;
Nor fancy me a goddess born,
Beware of the ideal.

Too soon, too soon, alas! thou'dst find,
  My birth-place not celestial,
And from an angel, I would sink
  Into a sad terrestrial.

Then let confiding faith be shown,
  And manly—honest feeling,
"A leal light heart" can never throb
  With ought that needs concealing.

THOUGHTS.

My bosom once rejoiced to treasure,
Hopes of many a joyous measure,
Ah! poor bosom, thou hast known,
What it was to find joy flown.

Once my heart beat proudly, brightly,
Beamed my eyes, more clearly, brightly.
Ah! poor heart thy peace is o'er,
Beams the sadden'd eye no more.

Life was once a bed of flowers,
Joy reposed in sunny bowers;
Life—thy buds were but a snare.
Thorns were hidden every where.

Heaven! I thought not of thy joys!
Pleas'd with this world's shining toys;
Now—but thee alone I prize,
Raise a suppliant to the skies.

TO THE MESSAGE BIRD.

Bird of beauty, whose bright plumage
Sparkles with a thousand dyes,
Soft thy note, and gay thy carol,
Tho' stern winter rules the skies.

First I knew thee by the sun-light
Of the summer's closing day—
Idly by the streamlet wand'ring,
Listening to thy vocal lay.

Joyfully I've hailed thy coming,
  By the prairie's spreading plain,
Or where southern roses blossom,
  Charmed by thy magic strain.

Com'st thou to me in the silence
  Of my snow-clad home to cheer,
Dost thou bear a message to me
  From the friend beloved and dear?

Welcome—for a leaf, sweet wand'rer,
  Thou hast plucked and borne, to me
Bringing many a thought of gladness
  'Mid a dream of melody.

THE EXILE'S LAMENT.

Breathe but those words, "beloved come,"
And, as the pilgrim to his shrine,
  The wild bird to its nest;
So will my willing spirit greet
Those words so welcome and so sweet,
  And seek with thee to rest.

The breeze that passeth o'er my brow
Perchance but late hath passed o'er thine;
  Oh! could it bear one tone
To cheer an Exile's weary lot,
Breathing, belov'd, and unforgot,
  I'm thine, and thine alone.

Toil would be sweet, with that dear voice
To sooth me, heedless—though the storm
  Were bursting o'er my head;
Those words, like music from afar,
Or light, shed from hope's guiding star,
  Would speak of days long fled.

Ah! no! of home nor joy it speaks;—
The cold blast chills my fainting form,
  The Exile's dream hath past!
Deserted—sad—with failing breath,
He asks one boon alone—come death,
  Thou true friend and the last.

THE REVERSE.

Life was to me a summer day,
So full of youth and bloom,
Of light and lovliness ; and earth,
A garden of perfume.

I knew not that those sunny hours
Could be by storms o'ercast ;
I did but dream that gentle showers
Would fall—too light to last.

And yet I've lived to see that sky
By tempests wildly riven :
To see earth's flow'rets fade and die,
Before the whirlwind driven.

To mourn, with anguish'd heart, the wreck
Of all that made life fair ;
To feel that roses oft may deck
The forehead of despair.

SONG.

Ah! Wisdom may speak from his bright open
page,
And look on young beauty with visage so sage,
But when Folly's sweet bells in the distance are
heard,
Believe, for I swear it, she'll not hear a word.

Wisdom speaks like a judge, and his speeches
are sound ;
His words are well chosen, his periods round ;
But when Folly, in rhyme, tells a maiden she's
fair,
Old Wisdom may grumble his words to the air.

Then say not that verse hath a rapid decline,
While live gentle women—while flows the rich
wine;
I'll woo in a song the sweet girl of my soul,
And the burden shall be—raise the ruby-tinged
bowl.

TO ——

Star of my fate ! my life—my love—my joy !
What endless toils thy weary hours employ !
What cares—what pleasures—win you thus to stay
Far from my heart, that chides thy long delay ?

The chilling winter lives but in the past,—
Soft swells its requiem on the moaning blast !
Exulting Zephyrs ride the passing gale,
And swell the canvass of the home-bound sail !

Lo ! to the moaning breeze my voice I lend ;
Ye Gods ! I cry ; Give back my wand'ring friend
If far from me, (by some slow winding stream,)
He loves 'mid nature's solitudes to dream,—
Or with the fisher's cunning art, uncoils
The willing reel, ensnaring in his toils,
(Won by the gaudy fly, or luscious bait,)
The giddy fish swift rushing to its fate ;—
Breathe thou, unto his heart, that once he joyed
In other arts, when love his thoughts employed !
Then the enchanting page, or converse gay,
Won him, all willingness, with me to stay.

Oh! say not he is false! that tale of wo—
Ye Gods!—in mercy to my heart, forego!
Tell me he lives! for me—for me alone!
Love lights his eyes, and breathes through every
tone.

Those beaming orbs, those stars of my own skies,
Whose votary, with'ring in their absence, dies,
Bid them illume, once more my lonely night,
Nor banish me from that sweet source of light.

STANZAS.

Oh! not to me, oh! not to me,
That look of cold disdain,
From others, I could calmly brook
The careless word, the chilling look—
But oh! from *thee*, 'tis pain.

The silver chord—the silver chord
When severed may unite
With other ties; but ah! when broke
The lute from whence those chords awoke,
It can no more delight.

As to the sun, the glorious sun,
The bending Persian prays—
And lingers till he views no more
Its light, nor ceases to adore,
In gloom, its parted rays.

So, o'er my heart, my faithful heart,
The love that budded there—
Still clings, as when in youth it clung;
For memory, constant memory flung,
With fond and anxious care,

So many thoughts—so many thoughts,
Of bliss, of joy, of pain—
When I would tear thee from my mind,
Her magic spells thine image bind—
The effort is in vain.

Then, not to me—oh! not to me
That look of cold disdain,
From others, I could calmly brook
The careless word, the chilling look—
But oh! from thee, 'tis pain.

TO ——

We may not break, beloved,
The spell around us thrown,
Until the silver chord is loosed
And hope, with life, hath flown.

Then think not absence ever
Can from my bosom take
A love unchangeable, should'st thou,
E'en thou—thy faith forsake.

Ah ! no—think not thus falsely ;
When grief hath dimmed thine eye,
And life, with all its cares, hath press'd
Too keenly—and too nigh,

That I could chide those tears,
Or thy deep grief condemn ;
Tho' from the oak each bough were shorn,
The vine twines round its stem.

Thus, should my love still lighten
The gloom of coming years,
Still faithful to my truth and thee,
Through sunshine and in tears.

DEATH OF OPECHANCANOUGH.

[*Indian Biography.*]

A monarch in captivity was dying—
And sad attendants round his death-bed stood;
He—the sole ruler o'er a numerous tribe,
A savage empire, won 'mid wilds and wood—
Like a spent lion in the strong snare lying;
Worn with long age and many a bloody strife,
Hopeless, o'erpower'd—the noble captive hailed
The dying close of a famed warrior's life.
Gone was the power to move each shrunken limb;
His heavy eyelids drooped—all powerless now;
Yet the fierce fire of those stern eyes still lay
Unquenchéd by age—beneath his lofty brow.
Wild murmurs broke from his attendants; him—
Their Chieftain loved,—was he not almost free;
In the dim passage to that dreamy land—
Wandering? Why call him back so frantically
The monarch bade them raise each heavy lid;
And, gazing sternly on a pale-faced crowd,
"Call the white chieftain of this hostile band,"
He said. Then came his victor; when aloud

The fierce old warrior—with stern sorrow chid
The heartless man, and said : "Had'st thou been led
Captive unto the red man's wigwam—he
Had saved from curious eyes thy dying bed."

TO GRACE ——.

Thou'rt in a fairy clime, sweet one,
'Mid the bright and lovliest thou,
Yet, a shade is o'er thy bosom cast,
And o'er thy sunny brow.

Dost thou pine for thine own far distant land,
With its forests vast and drear,
For the wild bird's call o'er the clear blue lake,
And the bounding of the deer ?

Or weep'st thou for a mother's form,
By thy lonely couch to kneel ;
Or the holy kiss of a father's love
On thy pale sweet brow to feel ?

Both, both ! though the wintry wind may sweep
O'er the forest in its pride ;

Though the echo of each sweet note may cease
The ruffled lake beside;

Though the deer no more with its graceful step
O'er the snow-clad hills may leap,
I pine, I pine for that far, far shore,
For my parent's voice I weep.

LOVE.

Love bringeth thoughts, that make their own distress,
It bringeth dreams, too, full of happiness,
And hopes, that fall like dew-drops o'er the rose,
Shedding sweet odours, even o'er life's close.

A deep, a dangerous delight it seems
To live on other's breath, a life of dreams—
When but a word, a look, a passing sigh
Can bring such blessedness—or misery.

An opening bud, a faded fallen leaf
Calleth back memories of joy or grief;
The wind that sweepeth wildly o'er the plain,
Whispers love's passionate farewell again.

'Tis better not to love; the heart can dwell
On other themes of happiness as well—
Let kindly faces gather round my hearth,
And cheer life's pilgrimage with song and mirth.

> " My spirit turns to thee, and, bird-like, flings
> Its best, its breath, its spring, and song o'er thee."

Nay, say not so, beloved—oh! do me not such wrong,—
I've loved you very fondly—I'm sure I've loved you long;
My bosom has a hidden fount—a fount of hope and love;
Affection deeply lies, but hope is sparkling far above.
Oh! do not cloud its cheerfulness, by deeming me untrue;
Hope, dimm'd, throws on poor love below, a sad and sombre hue.
Oh! give me back thine own sweet smile, thy look of careless glee,
When eyes are bright and smiles are light, life glides so cheerily.

My own—(they sound so pleasantly, those two
sweet little words,)
Far sweeter than the merry call of summer-wooing birds;
For, oh! a depth of tenderness is in their very
tone,
Whenever you have welcomed me, by calling me
thine own.
Still call me so, beloved—and now adieu, adieu,
'Tis pleasant writing those few lines to be perused by you;
Tho' worldly cares may weary thee—those toils
and troubles o'er—
Come rest upon a faithful heart, and never doubt
me more.

TO ———

Thy mellow voice is still upon mine ear,
Sweet as the murmuring of the distant brake,
Nature's wild melody, when soft and clear,
Light zephyr bids its harmony awake.

But changed, alas! thine eyes' deep tenderness,
To looks of cold indifference—careless, free;
It seem'd as if e'en memory had less
Of its sweet treasures, when I gazed on thee.

And is it thus the fond heart is repaid
For restless hours of watching and of grief?
For thoughts of thee, when low in sickness laid,
To whisper thy lov'd name seemed a relief.

Alas! that I might dream of hope once more,
Of love, that fleeted as a summer beam
On troubled waters—that a moment wore
Its sunny radience—oh, that I could dream!

But, no, it may not be, for we have met
As strangers meet; the careless smile and free—
The hand's cold touch—oh, said they not—
"forget
All that I vow'd—all that I was to thee?"

My dream is o'er, and on the whispering breeze,
Or in the song that bids the wood rejoice,
I'll trace no more thy word's sweet melodies,
Nor think that music speaketh with thy voice.

CONFESSIONS.

I speak in very bitterness, for I have deeply felt
The mock'ry of the hollow shrine at which my spirit knelt.
The weary hours—the restless nights—the mind in tumults toss'd,
Ambition—were thy gilded toys worth the sweet peace they cost?
Alas! alas! for woman's heart, 'tis an unworthy shrine,
To offer up the spirit's love—and, oh! unfit for mine.
Yet must I still the phantom seek, nor listen love's mild tone,
Breathed from lips whose eloquence I tremble whilst I own;
And I must learn to disavow the feelings of my soul—
To teach my throbbing heart to bow to reason's calm control;
To look with coldness on the brow, where love's bright seal is set—

To turn from passion's fervent vow, and struggle to forget;
And this is woman's destiny—a life of many cares—
A smiling brow above the gloom the aching bosom bears;
And her reward, a loneliness of spirit and of years.
No gentle hand her own to press—with sympathizing tears.
Her fair cheek pales beneath the chill the world hath round her cast;
Yet must she woman's fate fulfil, and struggle to the last;
E'en to the last—dissembler still—the tomb may not reveal
Her love's wild terror; nor despair break from the grave's cold seal.
And if I speak in bitterness—have I not deeply felt?
Aye, trembled—lest in tenderness my woman's heart should melt;

And I have bowed me to the ground, before ambition's shrine ;
Oh! holy love—warm, pure, and true—would I could bow at thine !

> " My first look on thy spotless spirit fell,
> And fate put forth its hand—inexorable—cold."
>
> SCHILLER.

I'LL dream no more ; let me go forth
Where the wild rose seeks its dwelling,
'Neath the green-wood shade in quiet laid
By the fountain gently swelling.

The fire of youth from my brow hath pas'd,
Tho' the minstrel spell is o'er me,
Yet the chords are jarred and the music marred,
Of the broken lute before me.

No hand again may touch its chords,
Or its loosened strings awaken :
Life's happy dreams, like its music, seems
A melody forsaken.

Forsaken—yet life's stream flows on,
  And it beareth on its foam
The wreck of towers, built in happier hours,
  When the spirit loved to roam.

And the murmuring of its restless wave,
  (For memory such thou art,)
Tho' its every tone be but a moan,
  Findeth echo in my heart.

I'll dream no more; dreams are not bliss,
  When the heart and lute are riven;
We can weave no spell despair to quell,
  'Till we forth the fiend have driven.

THE PACKET-SHIP ASHBURTON.

The gallant ship is riding free
  Upon the dancing wave,
Her snowy sails are filled—the breeze
  Its gentle impulse gave.

And brightly forth, beneath the sun,
  (Whilst white-foam wreathed around
Her graceful prow,) she glided, like
  A bride with chaplets crowned.

And the waves will kiss her daily,
  Wooing with the breath of morn,
And they'll aid her, whilst they greet her,
  As on her course she's borne.

How gracefully her white sails drooped,
  Ere freshly blew the breeze;
How proudly, when her canvass filled,
  She rode upon the seas.

* * * * * * *

The sun looks out from the blue sky,
  A glorious winter's sun,
The white cliffs in the distance rise,
  The hoped-for land is won.

Now gladly launch thy swiftest boat,
  Row onward to the strand;

Ye wand'rers from your native shore
  Step out upon the land.

A few brief hours—a few short weeks—
  Once more upon the main
Glideth that bold and gallant ship—
  She seeketh home again.

Her swift prow dasheth thro' the wave,—
  We smile, her sails to greet;
And welcome, with a sailor's love,
  The gallant ship so fleet.

THE COQUETTE.

Mary, dear Mary, oh! never say no,
But speak with thine own voice, so gentle and low,
And look in mine eyes with thine own of true blue,
Whilst you whisper—Oh! William, I dearly love you.

But Mary has turned from her wooer away—
She plucked the wild rose from its prickly spray,
The brier it wounded—Ah ! maiden, and thou
Hast wounded another—pale, pale is his brow.

And is it so, Mary ?—Heaven help me ! I go ;—
This moment of agony may you ne'er know !—
He sprang to his feet—and his look of farewell
Was on Mary's vain heart like a withering spell.

Some said, as a sailor afar he had sailed,
And her light form grew thinner, her rosy cheek
paled ;
The old mother sighed, for she well knew the
trace
Of death on her daughter's once beautiful face.

The summer hath passed—and the winter is
o'er,
Again spring is clust'ring the buds round the
door ;
Tho' balmy and sweet be the May's gentle breath
Poor Mary still withers, it brings to her—death.

The brier is blooming as when they last met,
But the eyes of a mother with tears are still wet;
It hath bloomed and hath faded, its pale leaves
are shed,
And William long weeps o'er the loved and the
dead.

TO THE MEMORY OF ONE OF THE SIGNERS OF THE INDEPENDENCE, BURIED BENEATH TRINITY CHURCH.

Thou askest me of thy sire, my boy—thine ancient sire, whose hand
Assisted in the mighty work that freed this glorious land.
They laid him in the ground, with many a tear
and prayer,
And the last of those that lov'd him, were
gathered humbly there;

They wept not for the patriot—what recked they of a name?—
They knew that he had gone, and what to him was fame:
But in the solitude of home—as years crept slowly on,
And time, with healing wing, had soothed the grief now calmly borne,
The memory of those gallant men, and he, their aged sire,
Kindled anew within their hearts, his pure and holy fire.

Thou asketh me, my boy—"Where lie the ashes of the dead?
Raised not his country, for that deed, the marble o'er his head?"
Aye; e'en a monument of art—of sculpture rich and rare:
Oh! never hath the young eye gazed on ought so wondrous fair.
But, to the One Eternal is that holy structure reared,—

He, unto whom thy grand-sire bowed—the loved,
and yet the feared;
And when thou bendeth on thy knee, and pray-
eth for God's grace,
Forget not him whose aged form lies 'neath that
holy place.

CHILDHOOD'S PRAYER.

It is a pure and holy thing,
Young childhood's simple prayer,
So little of man's worldliness,
So much of Heaven seems there.
Their eyes upraised and small hands clasped,
While dwell their lips upon
Their Savior's words, (when agonized)
"Father, thy will be done."

Ah! mother, gaze upon thy child,
Thou know'st he now is pure;
How much of misery—of crime—
May that young heart endure!

The first of his brief life hath gone,—
  As a sweet dream it pass'd;
Oh! think not in thy hopefulness
  Such blessed days will last;
For Sorrow meets man in his course,
  Blighting each promised joy;
And moody, in his noon-tide hour,
  Becomes the buoyant boy.

Or Pleasure, with her winning smile,
  Points to her fragrant bowers,—
Deeply of Circe's cup he drinks,
  And strews the brim with flowers.
The poison works!—ah! mother! see
  Thy young, thy cherished son,
Pale—drooping—dying! Life hath past,
  And pleasure's course is run.

Must it be thus? No; let us hope
  Those youthful prayers may rise—
Thus humbly blended with thine own—
  "Sweet incense to the skies."

That God may send his blessing down
  Upon the trusting one,
And guard from sorrow and from guilt
  Thy pure and only son.

THE CONSUMPTIVE.

I cannot rest with a breaking heart,
  Till I rest within my grave;
Vain is the leech's healing art,
  He hath no power to save.

I am passing to that "better land"
  Where the weariest soul hath peace;
Kind friends, why pray to stay the hand
  That bids my torture cease?

Oh! bring me to my Savior's love,
  "Father, who art in Heaven,"
And raise my erring soul above
  The love to which 'twas given.

Her lips, half parted, were in prayer,
Low bent the graceful head;
Her words they seemed to echo there,
E'en when her soul had fled.

The story, 'twas a simple one,
Of loving feelings borne,
Till passion's own intensity
Had the youug dreamer worn.

In silence and in solitude
It preyed within her breast,
A secret guarded faithfully,
And scarce to Heaven confessed.

There was one mourner at her tomb,
A stranger seemed he here;
All marvell'd how his strong frame shook,
When standing by her bier.

And when the earth had closed her in,
And the last prayer was said,
They heard him mutter, "Would that I
Were buried with the dead!"

None knew him but the aged man
  Who wept above his child,
And saw in him a neighbor's son—
  A reckless youth and wild—

Companion of her childhood's years,—
  Lovers, 'twas said, in youth;
Alas! for man's inconstancy,
  For woman's dying truth.

PHILOSOPHY OF THE STARS.

The Heavens are calm and the night serene,
Look out, fair girl, 'tis a fairy scene,
And mark how the moon, with that star so fair,
Still wend their way through the fields of air.

And ever 'tis thus, when the skies above,
Are lit with the moon's pale light of love;
Still pressed to her side with a jealous care,
Like a favorite lover, that star is there.

Yes, gaze! 'tis the star of my natal hour,
And, born 'neath its trembling ray,
Was the spirit of bliss, who on earth hath power,
And in Heaven an holier sway.

Then think of them, love, as a glorious boon,
As a type of that spirit given,
And gaze on that star and the calmer moon
As an emblem of Hope and Heaven.

"There have been roses round my lute, but now
I must forsake them for the cypress bough."

THE FESTIVAL.

(From an Ancient Song of the Troubadours, or Trouvèrès.)

The sound of merry minstrelsy breathes from yon lofty hall,
Light-moving footsteps glide along re-echoing music's call,
And many a young and joyous heart beats 'neath the silken dress,
That shadows yet reveals so much of maiden loveliness.

But she, the fairest and the loved—amid that joyous throng,
Whose life seemed but one pleasant dream of perfume and of song,
Seemed weary; with impatient look she glanced her eyes around—
Ah! like the Ark's fair Dove—no green, nor resting place they found.

Gone was the echo of the dance—fled mirth and minstrelsy—
Nought but a clear and placid stream, could that sweet lady see,
No sound, but sounds of tenderness, from one, whose manly tone
And noble bearing, won the heart that beat for him alone;
And he was bending on his knee, right by that pleasant stream.
(Oh! wonder not in grandeur's hall, came such a simple dream,
For Love will enter in as well as in the humble cot—

Then wealth seems poor and power is vain, and
worldly thoughts forgot.)

A sudden spell hath caught her ;—now she
wakes from her wild trance,
The brightest in the glittering throng—the gayest
in the dance.
For who may read that lady's eye—and mark the
secret there?
Or trace the serpent's trail where flowers and per-
fume showered are?
You've marked the blossom on the bush, the leaf
upon the tree,
And knew not that the hidden worm was work-
ing silently ;
You've seen, e'er from the tree it fell, the leaf's
rich gorgeous hue,
Nor recked that summer ne'er again, with its
sweet healing dew,
Can bring the beauty to the bud—the freshness to
the leaf.
So fades the cheek—so withers all, beneath the
touch of grief.

And love, all fearful in its course—a love that
might not bless,
Had thrown its shadow o'er her brow, and dim-
med its loveliness.

* * * * * * * * * *

Ah! tear the serpent from thine heart, the wreath
from off thy brow,
And in thy closet bend the knee with a more holy
vow;
And clothe thine heart with purity, with penance
and with prayer;
Sow not the whirlwind, reap not thou repent-
ance and despair.

THE BLOODY RUN.

A party of soldiers were attacked by Indians at a stream called, from the circumstances of the fight, "The Bloody Run."

In the bosom of the mountain,
Where the ling'ring moonbeams lay,
Calm in their placid beauty,
Like an infant tired of play,

Just where the last shade parted
  When the sun had sunk to sleep,
A torrent wildly darted
  From a high and rocky steep.

Around, in ambush crouching,
  Were hid an Indian foe,
With their deadly hatchets gleaming
  'Neath the furze and brushwood low;
Like the lurking panther stealing
  O'er the forest to its prey,
Well hidden by the cedar,
  The treach'rous Indians lay.

What sound hath broke the silence
  Of this wild and savage lair?
The merry notes of drum and fife,
  With banners floating fair,
And martial steps all treading
  The steep and rugged way;
Their bayonets glitter brightly
  In the moonbeams glancing ray.

O'er the mountain's lofty bosom
  With wearied steps and slow
They come—now thread the valley,
  Now reach the water's flow.
They dip their way-worn bonnets
  In the wave, to cool their thirst,
When, with whoop and yell, the Indians
  From their ambush madly burst.

Now circles high the hatchet,
  Now gleams the sharpen'd knife ;
Like deer at gaze, each victim
  Gives up his panting life.
They sink, they bleed, they struggle,
  The stream is tinged with gore,
And those who stooped to drink it
  The waters have passed o'er.

One moment, and they rally,
  On the treach'rous foeman turn,
And to revenge their comrades,
  With stern resolve they burn ;
For days the foe are hunted

Through the forest and the dell,
And for their murder'd brethren
Full five score Indians fell.

The peasant, when he wanders
Past that scene of blood and strife,
Half trembles in the moonlight,
Lest he see the gleaming knife ;
Though the Indians long have perish'd
On the mountains wooded breast,
Yet he deems their spirits linger
Where their mould'ring bones have rest.
And he trembles, as the shadows
From the fast-receding sun
Are gathering—and, in terror,
He leaves the Bloody Run.

THE BACKWOODSMAN'S TALE.

" And in a voice of solemn joy that awed
Echo into oblivion, he said—"

Heaven smiled propitiously upon the land
My fathers won, and the Creator's hand

Conspicuous shone ; for there, luxuriant fields
A wealthy harvest to the farmer yields,
And shady groves, with cooling streams unite
To temper with their freshness Heaven's warm
light.
Fruits, flowerets, herbs profusely scattered o'er
Bade e'en the savage, Nature's God adore—
To lowly bow, and 'neath each shady bower
By nature softened, own a higher power.
Creation's beauties filling every sense,
He asks the cause, and owns th' Omnipotence.

And I was blest ! my child—our only one—
Sought my caress at eve, when toil was done ;
Whilst my own Mary dressed the cleanly board
With wholesome food, and fruits delicious stored.
Each Sabbath morn, at the first dawn of day,
By the pure light we rose, for we could pray
To the blessed giver of content, as well
'Neath the wide Heavens as by the chapel bell.
The grateful heart a response still may find
In the fair fields—or breathing on the wind.

The Indian tribes, by treaties, had been won
Afar to wander—where the setting sun
Claims as his own the vallies, fields and wood
Glowing beneath—of light a glorious flood.
Not then had murder loosed her fiendish train,
But peace and plenty ruled the fertile plain.

One stilly eve, we sat within the porch,
Watching our child—as, eager for the torch
Of the fire-fly, that, circling round his head,
Flashed tiny lightning, after it he sped,
(My fearless boy) bounding within the gloom
Of the deep forest. Faded then the bloom
From his fond mother's cheek—"Oh, haste!" she cried,
"The prowling wolves within the forest bide;
No later than this morn their steps were nigh
Our cottage door." I listened to her cry,
And sought the child with undefined alarm—
A fearful trembling—could our boy meet harm
In the dark wood? Hark! was it Mary's scream?
I flew to meet my child lest she should deem

Some evil had befallen ; all was still
As the calm tomb—when, suddenly, a shrill
And bitter cry rose 'mid the solitude,
And a bright light illuming where I stood,
Showed me my boy—dead—dead! Oh! God! oh! God!
His fair locks trampled in the bloody sod.

I do not rave—nay, stare not thus aghast,
That vision shakes my soul, but it hath past ;
Weeping I bore him to our once calm cot ;
He, the young blessing of our lonely lot
Had yielded his pure soul ; I was alone !
And, mourning, I retraced my steps—when shone
A fiercer light—and yells, as if were hurled
A spirit of the tortured on the world ;
Curdled my blood ;—I saw the flaming torch
Upon my dwelling ; by the crumbling porch
Stood the dark savage—demon—murderous foe,
Aiming o'er Mary's head the deadly blow.
Thank Heaven ! my arm was strong ; he fell,
Pierced by my bullet—how, I scarce can tell.
Mary was saved ; but, senseless, from the ground

I raised her, and the first low sound
Was, "My dear boy—oh! bring him to me now;
Let us together to our Maker bow.
Are we not saved? Come husband let us pray!"
And starting from my bosom, where she lay,
Ere I could break to her the dreadful tale,
She saw the murdered child; one bitter wail
Burst from her lips; then quietly she knelt,
And wiped his brow; and his stilled bosom felt,
And gazed on him; alas! her reason passed
E'en as she gazed; upon them both the blast
Had fallen—ever, from that hour,
Speechless, she was—a pale and dying flower
Wrecked by the wintry wind—her form
Felt not the glowing summer's breathing warm;
Yet still she lived, if such can be called breath—
This lingering 'twixt the arms of love and death;
Dead to all here—patient, but still; so still,
That e'en the sufferer's death were lesser ill.

And years had passed—alas! she could not die,
But still breathed on—the spring-time now was
nigh.

And Mary sat with me within the door,
For she the wintry months had lingered o'er,
Brooding with moody lips—mute, startful, hot—
A maniac look—that tale had o'er her shot.
I turned upon the sufferer to look—
Her frame with all-unwonted tremors shook,
And the long-absent blood rushed to her cheek;
She wept—oh! did I dream?—My Mary, speak,
I cried.—She met my gaze
With all the fondness of our happier days.
My husband, murmured she; my child, my child!
Lay me with him! then, kissing me, she smiled,
And, bending her meek head upon my breast,
So died.—I laid her where she prayed to rest.

And through the pathless prairies, unseen
'Till now, by man, a wanderer I've been.
Each year I seek their grave. Stranger, I pray
That soon my aged bones in peace may lay
With theirs so loved. * * * *

"THE LAST ERRAND OF THE INDIAN CHIEF 'BALD EAGLE.'"*

Speed on, speed on, no sound is borne
  Upon the troubled wave;
The bark hath sped—its steersman wan,
  No cheering answer gave.

On, on it sped—I trow the dead
  Fear not the current strong,
No oar propell'd, and yet it fled,
  A fearful thing along.

And high above the ravens scream
  In eddying circle round,
The wild deer, starting from the stream,
  Springs with a startled sound.

The "Bashkwa" wheels above the wood,
  The gloom is deep'ning now,
The doomed bark, safe o'er the flood,
  Hath passed with steady prow:

* C. Hoffinan's "Winter in the West."

Step out, step out, brave mariner,
  Thy wonted goal is won,
And soft thy couch of yielding fur,
  Come, rest—thy toils are done.

He spoke not, looked not once around,
  His fearful errand 's sped ;
The death-bark touched upon the land,
  They gazed upon the dead.

Revenge! revenge! the war-whoop sound!
  The mystic wampum weave,
Tear the red hatchet from the ground,
  Thus, shall thy warriors grieve.

Let burning brand and bloody blade
  Avenge our chieftain's wrong ;
The light turf on his corse they laid,
  Then raised their battle song.

* * * * * * * * * *

Years have passed on, yet in the gloom,
  The lonely settler fears
To meet that bark of death and doom,
  As on its shadow steers.

THE BLASTED OAK.

Dark on the heath the night gloom fell,
Loud sighed the wind ; with fitful spell
The light'ning glared around,
And meeting clouds, with angry roar,
The burthen of the tempest bore,
Far o'er the trembling ground.

Hark ! heard ye not, 'mid torrents borne,
The echo of a distant horn
Upon the moaning blast ?
And clatt'ring hoofs as if, with speed,
For life, for life spurred on a steed—
It comes, and now 't hath past,

With bloody spur, and frantic mien—
Too well the rider's haste, I ween,
Of crime, of terror spoke ;
And ever and anon he threw
A fearful glance, where lonely grew
An old and gnarled oak.

For 'neath that leafless trunk hath lain
The mould'ring corse, of one long slain;
(Oh, God! can such things be?)
The rider spurred his courser on;
"Oh! for the blessed beam of morn
To light me cheerily!"

On, on the madden'd courser fled,
His snorting nostrils speak his dread—
With visage ghastly pale
The rider spurred;—"My gallant steed
Why faulter at thy master's need?
Why tremble thus, and quail?

Avaunt, ye spirits of the slain.
My horn shall gaily sound again,
To bid yon loiterers haste."
He said; and wound a trembling blast—
Started the horse, as, moaning, pass'd,
A shadow o'er the waste.

"'Tis he!"—the trembling murderer cries,
"Oh, God!—I see his pleading eyes—
That wide and bleeding gash:—

Hah ! ha !—'tis but a shadow, born
Of clouds—(such oft the earth hath worn ;)
  Scared by the lightning's flash !

Down came Heaven's bolt—a forked light
Play'd round the tree ; and, by the bright
  And vivid flame it cast,
I saw the murderer, writhing, fall ;
Then closed around night's gloomy pall,
  And louder moaned the blast.

THE COMBAT.

His helmet is cloven, his lance shivered lies,
His white plumes are tinged with the battle's red
    dyes ;
In vain his bright corslet—the foe's deadly thrust
Through the links of his mail-covered body hath
    burst.

Now yield thee, Sir Knight, fair Oneila thy
    bride !
Her beauty shall cheer me—her domains are
    wide ;

That bright flower of love I would wreath round
my soul—
Then yield her, the prize, to thy victor's control.

Faint, faint felt the knight, and his head drooped
low,
'Till it bent to the rise of his steel saddle-bow ;
The bright sun seemed shaded, and fast o'er
the ground
The lengthening shadows were gathering round.

Yield, yield thy Oneila, thine arm, boy, is
weak—
The soft down is short on thy fair youthful
cheek ;
Young beauty from thee no protection can claim ;
Fame breathes not one blast at the sound of thy
name.

The Heavens were purple with sunset's last glow,
As young Theodore turned from his dark-visor'd
foe ;
He thought of his lordly and far-distant tower—
Of her, his young bride, in her desolate bower ;

And his life-blood flowed faster!—Oh! who would defend
His bride, from the arts of his false perjured friend?

"False craven!"—he shouted; dilated his eye,
As he uttered the words of his dread prophecy;—
"Thy bones soon shall whiten on Palestine land;
Nay, think not of home, thou wilt ne'er reach its strand:
The plague is upon thee—I see it—I feel!
Its pangs are far keener than glittering steel;
Onelia, Oneila—to thee, love, I come—
We will rove by the cool-flowing fountains—our home
Is fair, love," he murmured.—In death now recline
The victor and vanquished, in far Palestine.

DEATH AND THE WARRIOR.

Away to the battle—the foe onward pour—
Away, my fleet courser, I ne'er needed more
Thy speed and thy courage—on, on to the fight;
One glance, at the onset, were worth a whole life.

"Oh! stay thy fleet steed," said a voice in his
ear,
"A foe is approaching—his footsteps are near;
Not low on the gory-stained field thou wilt lie;
Oh, warrior, prepare thee! this moment thou'lt
die."

The warrior he started—and, lo! at his side,
In loose sable garment, a horseman did ride;
No weapon displayed he—no word did he speak,
Yet the red color blanched on the warrior's
cheek.

His eyes on the knight he so steadily turned,
Like bright glowing coals, in their sockets they
burn'd;

Oh! he who could gaze, undismayed, on their
gleam,
Was a warrior in feeling and bearing, I deem.

Then answered the knight:—"So help me, St.
Bride!
Whilst my lance, still unbroken, I bear by my
side;
My helmet and shield to no foe will I yield,
Whilst my heart breathes a gasp on the blood-
stained field."

The warrior hath spoken, and calmly he gazed,
While the sable-clothed horseman his hand
slowly raised;
"Not low on the gory-stained field thou wilt lie;
Oh, warrior, prepare thee! this moment thoul't
die."

"And must it be so, then? Death, art thou so
near?
I shun thee not—phantoms the coward may
fear;

'Mid the battle I hoped to have breathed my
last sigh ;
Now farewell, my country—farewell, ye bright
sky."

Lo ! his helmet and shield in the dust they are
strown,
His fleet steed afar o'er the wide plain hath
flown ;
The phantom he vanished in darkness and
gloom,
And they bear the cold corse of the knight to the
tomb.

QUEEN MARY'S ESCAPE FROM LOCH-LEVEN CASTLE.

The moon looks down on lake and lea,
O'er wood and ruined tower,
And tinges, with its silvery light,
The Lady's lofty bower.

No light, save from the moonbeam's ray,
  Upon the casement streams;
The flame hath to the socket burnt,
  The gentle lady dreams.

Not then so darkly was it wont
  On former eves to be;
Bright lights, then, from the casement stream'd,
  And merry minstrelsy.

And gallant knights within that hall,
  Sighed for a smiling glance
From her, the loveliest in the land,
  The royal dame of France.

But now she rests in captive thrall,
  Fair Scotia's beauteous queen;
A brighter gem hath never beam'd
  In diadem, I ween.

Oh! shame on Scotland's chivalry,
  On Britain's nobles, shame;
Why rest their scabbards on the blade,
  When weeps so fair a dame?

She dreams, perchance, of grievous wrongs,
Of manhood's blighted truth,
Or fondly of her own lov'd France
And happy days of youth—

Or sadly muses o'er her lot,
With pensive step, and slow,
Wandering beneath that vaulted dome,
A beauteous form of woe.

The moon shines brightly o'er the scene,
And, by its mellow'd light,
Upon the ivy'd casement rests
An arm of ivory white.

And cautiously a female form
From that rude turret leant,
With stealthy glance, and anxious look
Upon the waters bent.

There is a ripple on the lake,
A sound upon the air,
And yet no breeze the waters stir,
The midnight sky is fair.

The moon looks out on lake and lea,
  And o'er that gloomy tower;—
Lady, arise, no longer weep,
  Propitious is the hour.

I see a noble manly form
  A shallop lightly skim,
And now it touches on the shore—
  Brave Douglas, it is him.

The turret door is quickly won,
  The warder he doth sleep,
And other hands now hold the key,
  And ope that dismal keep.

Queen Mary on the threshold stands,
  One startled look she cast
Upon the tower; her utter'd thought—
  "Heaven grant it be the last!"

She turned, and with gentle tone,
  "Brave Douglas, in my need,
Thou hast preserved a wretched one,
  Heaven's blessing on the deed.

The captive Mary yet may prove
  Her gratitude, but now—
Thanks—the poor guerdon she bestows,
  Tears and a happy brow!"

The Douglas bent with reverence low,
  Then, with a kindly haste,
He whispered, "On, my sovereign,
  The precious moments waste."

On the slight shallop's prow she stepp'd
  "Farewell, ye towers," she cried;
"Oh! Douglas, but for thee, perchance
  Within these walls I'd died."

"Susojos a mis ojos
Miven atentos,
Y, callando se dicen
Sus sentimentos,
Cosa es bien eavas,
Qua sin habaose entienden
Nuestros dos almas."

TO ——

It told me thou wert all my own—
(My gentle one)—that voiceless tone—

Dost thou forget the day
When gazing fondly in thine eyes,
I saw, with rapturous surprise,
Young love half hidden lay?
Blush not—that from thine eyes was told
A tale thy lips would deem too bold.

Nor e'er, sweet one, deny the tale
Once whispered 'neath the drooping veil
Of thine eyes' fringed lid?
But turn once more their tender gaze,
As in those early joyous days,
Ere by cold prudence chid.
Ah! treacherous lips, why thus deny
What's written in that tell-tale eye?

www.ingramcontent.com/pod-product-compliance
Lightning Source LLC
LaVergne TN
LVHW021406110826
845150LV00007B/1803

* 9 7 8 1 4 2 5 5 1 2 0 0 2 *